Cambridge Elements ≡

Elements in Metaphysics
edited by
Tuomas E. Tahko
University of Bristol

ABSTRACT OBJECTS

David Liggins
University of Manchester

Shaftesbury Road, Cambridge CB2 8EA, United Kingdom

One Liberty Plaza, 20th Floor, New York, NY 10006, USA

477 Williamstown Road, Port Melbourne, VIC 3207, Australia

314–321, 3rd Floor, Plot 3, Splendor Forum, Jasola District Centre, New Delhi – 110025, India

103 Penang Road, #05–06/07, Visioncrest Commercial, Singapore 238467

Cambridge University Press is part of Cambridge University Press & Assessment, a department of the University of Cambridge.

We share the University's mission to contribute to society through the pursuit of education, learning and research at the highest international levels of excellence.

www.cambridge.org
Information on this title: www.cambridge.org/9781009467858

DOI: 10.1017/9781009241373

First published 2024

A catalogue record for this publication is available from the British Library.

ISBN 978-1-009-46785-8 Hardback
ISBN 978-1-009-24140-3 Paperback
ISSN 2633-9862 (online)
ISSN 2633-9854 (print)

Abstract Objects

Elements in Metaphysics

DOI: 10.1017/9781009241373
First published online: February 2024

David Liggins
University of Manchester

Author for correspondence: David Liggins, david.liggins@manchester.ac.uk

Abstract: Philosophers often debate the existence of such things as numbers and propositions, and say that if these objects exist, they are abstract. But what does it mean to call something 'abstract'? And do we have good reason to believe in the existence of abstract objects? This Element addresses those questions, putting newcomers to these debates in a position to understand what they concern and what are the most influential considerations at work in this area of metaphysics. And it also provides advice on which lines of discussion promise to be the most fruitful.

Keywords: abstract, concrete, metaphysics, nominalism, platonism

ISBNs: 9781009467858 (HB), 9781009241403 (PB), 9781009241373 (OC)
ISSNs: 2633-9862 (online), 2633-9854 (print)

Contents

1 Introduction to this Element

The debate over the existence of abstract objects is like a complex landscape. In this Element, I will sketch out the lie of the land; I will draw attention to some significant features that a newcomer might miss; I will point out what seem to me dead ends; and I will indicate some paths that deserve further exploration. This will be a personal – even idiosyncratic – introduction to the abstract objects debate. It is intended not as a bland, neutral summary but as a contribution to this field of research. The contribution lies as much in my selection of material as in what I say about it.

It is appropriate for an introduction to be selective. Because an Element has a strict word limit, I have been extremely selective indeed. There are many works relevant to the abstract objects debate which I do not mention here. That does not mean I think them unworthy of attention.

I have been exploring this landscape for over twenty years. Investigating the existence of abstract objects has been richly rewarding: I hope this Element will inspire the reader to join in the exploration and to share the rewards.

The notion of abstractness figures in a wide range of philosophical debates. I hope this this Element will also be helpful to those who draw on the notion in passing. It should help them be aware of the complexities that surround it, even if they do not need to foreground them in their work.

I begin by talking about the definition of 'abstract object', and which side in the debate over the existence of abstract objects bears the burden of proof. Then I go on to consider arguments for and against their existence. From Section 3 onwards, I focus on three debates: the existence of numbers, the existence of propositions, and the existence of properties.

There is no consensus on whether numbers, propositions, or properties exist. Indeed, there is no consensus on whether there are abstract objects at all. In Section 5, I offer an explanation of the persistence of disagreement over the existence of abstract objects, by reflecting on the arguments I have discussed.

2 Introduction to the Debate

2.1 What Does 'Abstract Object' Mean?

In the debate over the existence of abstract objects, the word 'object' is used in different ways by different philosophers. In the sense that is important for introducing the topic, 'object' simply means 'thing' or 'entity'. In this sense of 'object', an object is not a special type of thing: everything is an object. If we discover that abstract objects exist, then we can debate what type of thing they are. But the more fundamental question is whether there are any abstract objects at all.

The debate over the existence of abstract objects therefore belongs to the part of metaphysics known as 'ontology', in which we try to find out what exists. There are well-known challenges to the legitimacy of ontological inquiry; I will ignore them here (see Chalmers 2009 for a survey). Similarly, some philosophers maintain that there is more to reality than what exists. They claim that there are some things which do not exist (see e.g. Parsons 1980). Here I will presuppose that what there is and what exists are the same.

There is much more to be said about 'abstract'. The term has no standard definition: philosophers sometimes claim to be repeating the standard definition, but the definitions they give are all different! Often philosophers use the term without introducing what they mean by it. Since 'abstract' is a technical term which different philosophers use in different ways, it doesn't make sense to debate which meaning is the correct one. There are simply different ways of using the term (Rosen 2009: Section 'Introduction'). However, a closely related question is worth considering: which way of using the term is the most fruitful?

To answer that question, we should begin by asking which way of using the term is most popular. When we engage in 'abstract object'-talk, we should try to mean the same as the other participants in the debate, or miscommunication will result. Also, we should bear in mind what sorts of objects are commonly thought of as clearly abstract and clearly not abstract: if our way of using the term does not respect those classifications, that is evidence that we have failed to latch on to the prevailing usage. When discussing the meaning of 'abstract' it is convenient to write as if all the candidates for being abstract or not abstract exist. That saves writing 'if they exist' all the time. So I will follow that policy for the remainder of this section.

Material objects, such as chairs, are commonly thought of as clearly not abstract. Numbers are commonly thought of as clearly abstract. By 'number' here I do not mean physical inscriptions, such as the numbers on the dial of my watch, but the objects to which these inscriptions refer.

Historically, a prominent way of introducing the notion of abstractness was in terms of a psychological operation whereby we 'abstract' away from some differences and focus on similarities (Rosen 2009: Section 'The Way of Abstraction'). But now abstractness is commonly introduced in terms of causality and spatio-temporal location. Call something 'acausal' if it does not take part in causal interactions. The notion of abstractness is often now introduced along these lines:

(D1) Something is abstract iff it is acausal and lacks spatio-temporal location.

Popular variations replace 'acausal' with 'causally impotent' or 'lacks causal power': on these definitions, abstract objects do not take part in causal interactions because they cannot. That difference is probably not very significant, because there is little plausibility to the thought that good candidates for being abstract objects are capable of causal interaction but somehow never do so. For instance, if we said that numbers can start fires, then we would be under pressure to explain why they never do so. It is neater to say that they can't.

Within the philosophy of mathematics, it is common to hold that numbers are acausal and tables are not. But many philosophers working on causation would say that only events are causes, so numbers and tables all cause nothing. If that is right, then we need to explain how some non-events can count as causally active even though they are not causes. (Here I echo Rosen 2009, Section 'The Causal Inefficacy Criterion'.)

The phrase 'lacks spatio-temporal location' raises deep complexities. Philosophers seldom explain what they mean when they use it. Does something that lacks a location in space automatically count as lacking spatio-temporal location? If so, then the 'temporal' part is redundant. So presumably this is not what is meant.

Abstract objects are sometimes characterised as 'beyond' or 'outside' time. But this talk is puzzling: it is not clear how to cash out these metaphors. Believers in abstract objects think that they exist now. It is natural to think that numbers have always existed and will always exist. On this view, numbers are especially old and especially long-lasting objects. But that need not mean that they are 'outside' time in any sense. Perhaps they occupy time in the same way as, for instance, chairs do – they just occupy it for an especially long period. The same goes for many other abstract objects. So the notion of being 'outside' time needs fleshing out; and the claim that abstract objects are 'outside' time in this sense will then need defending.

Philosophers of religion draw a distinction between sempiternality and eternality which might be useful here. To be 'sempiternal' is to exist at all moments of time. 'Eternal' is harder to define; there is a great deal of discussion of how best to do so and whether the notion really makes sense. (Stump and Kretzmann 1981: 430 introduce 'eternality' as 'the condition of having eternity as one's mode of existence', and go on to mount a classic defence of its coherence.) What is clear is that eternality is meant to be an alternative to sempiternality. Philosophers who are attracted to the idea that abstract objects are 'outside' time could draw on this debate in order to flesh out the idea and test it.

Perhaps the idea that some abstract objects are 'outside' or 'beyond' time can be clarified and defended. But it is unlikely that this could be true of all abstract objects, because some of them seem to be created by human activity. Consider *Pride and Prejudice* – not individual physical copies, but the novel itself of which these are copies. That is plausibly an abstract object; and before we start thinking systematically about the metaphysics of fiction, we are strongly inclined to say that it came into existence only when Jane Austen created it. Numbers may well have existed since the dawn of time, but nineteenth-century novels probably not. Abstract objects created by human activity are not even sempiternal, so they will have little chance of being 'beyond' time.

This example shows that, even if we want to say that some abstract objects are 'beyond' time, it is unwise to build the idea of being 'beyond' time into the definition of 'abstract'. It also shows that the notion of sempiternity is of limited use here (Hale 1987: 48–9 makes a similar point). Perhaps some abstract objects – numbers, for example – are sempiternal. But it is unwise to make it a matter of definition that all abstract objects exist sempiternally.

Most definitions do neither of those things. But many of them incorporate the idea of lacking a spatio-temporal location, which remains to be clarified. It is notable that in the contemporary debate over the existence of abstract objects, the notion of time plays only a minor role (Baker 2003 is a notable exception). Many of the arguments would look just the same if 'abstract' were defined as follows:

(D2) Something is abstract iff it is acausal and lacks spatial location.

I conclude that building a temporal concept into the definition of 'abstract' is more trouble than it's worth.

Things that lack a spatial location are sometimes said to be 'outside space'. But this is a dangerous metaphor: it encourages the thought that abstract objects are infinitely far away from us, in some 'abstract realm'. Because abstract objects lack a spatial location, they are not the sort of things that stand at a distance to other things. They are neither close nor far away: such concepts do not apply. As Rosen (1993: 152) points out, abstract objects are not 'elsewhere' but 'nowhere'.

Indeed, we can go further and point out that what is important here is not the idea of lacking a spatial location, but that of lacking a *particular* spatial location. Perhaps numbers are spread out through the whole of space: we cannot link them to particular locations, because each one of them is everywhere. That option is seldom discussed. I suspect it would leave the debate much as it is.

As I said, numbers are often thought of as clear cases of abstract objects, and material objects, such as chairs, as clear cases of objects that are not abstract. We should check that (D2) classifies these cases correctly. Let us start with numbers.

No-one ever makes their food more delicious by sprinkling into the saucepan some numbers, and no-one is ever rushed to hospital after a nasty collision with the square root of minus one. It's not just that there is no empirical evidence that such things ever happen; rather, we are confident that no such things ever happen, even without checking the empirical evidence. That's because we think of numbers as the sort of things that cannot be sprinkled, tasted, or collided with. We think of numbers as acausal.

Mathematics teachers do not take their pupils on school trips to get close to numbers. They do not even try to. We never describe numbers as being in a particular place; and it would be ludicrous to claim that π is moving slowly south-west. In other words, we do not think of numbers as being the sorts of things that are spatially located.

So our ordinary thinking about numbers portrays them as acausal and lacking spatial location. Until a sufficiently powerful challenge to our ordinary thinking arises, (D2) tells us that numbers are abstract. Since numbers are paradigms of the abstract, that is the right result.

Tables, on the other hand, are both spatially located and causally active. There is one in this room and it is reflecting light into my eyes right now. So (D2) tells us that tables are not abstract – again, the right result.

From here on, when I call something 'abstract', I will mean that in the sense given by (D2). For brevity and variety, philosophers sometimes borrow from Latin and call abstract objects 'abstracta' (singular: 'abstractum').

Many different things are probably abstracta. The following are plausibly thought of as acausal and lacking spatial location, hence abstract: games (e.g. chess); languages (e.g. Swedish); concepts (e.g. the concept of a triangle); theories (e.g. Newtonian mechanics); fictions (e.g. *Hamlet*); musical works (e.g. Beethoven's First Symphony); biological species (e.g. the King Penguin); recipes (e.g. for Peach Melba); and possible worlds. Of course, for any object, there is room for debate over whether it really is abstract.

Often we do not know enough about an object to be sure whether it counts as abstract. Not all mathematical entities are clearly abstract. Consider the singleton set of Edinburgh (written '{Edinburgh}') – that is, the set whose only member is Edinburgh. It is a matter of debate whether this object is located in Scotland, or not spatially located at all. If we decide {Edinburgh} is spatially located, we cannot say it is abstract. We should not assume that all sets lack a location, or that all sets have a location. Perhaps some sets, such as {Edinburgh}, are spatially located, whereas other sets, such as the empty set, are not. There is also a good question about whether {Edinburgh} is acausal. Is {Edinburgh} causally active? Or is it something causally inactive that contains as a member something causally active? What we say about this will have implications for whether to count {Edinburgh} as abstract.

It is common to take properties as clear examples of abstracta. But in fact it is controversial whether these entities meet the conditions for counting as abstract. There is a long-standing debate about the location of properties: are they where their instances are, or nowhere at all? Perhaps redness is where the red things are – or perhaps it's nowhere at all (see Oliver 1996: 25–33). Only those who deny properties spatial locations can claim properties are abstract. While the debate over the location of properties is unresolved, we should draw back from claiming that properties are abstract objects.

Propositions, too, are frequently classed as clear examples of abstract objects. But whether we say they are abstract depends partly on what we say about their nature. Consider the influential Russellian account of propositions. According to that account, propositions are tuples, some of which have chairs among their members. Is that enough to locate those propositions? If it is, then they are not abstract. Unless we have a good reason to deny that such tuples lack a spatial location, or to reject the Russellian account of propositions, we should keep an open mind about whether propositions are abstract. (On defining 'abstract', Lewis 1986: Section 1.7 and Rosen 2009 are essential reading.)

2.2 The Abstract/Concrete Distinction

So far I have just talked about whether objects are abstract or not. It is now time to bring in the notion of concreteness. As with 'abstract', many authors leave it unclear precisely what they mean by 'concrete', especially when they use the term in passing.

Abstract objects are contrasted with concrete ones: philosophers agree that nothing could be both, and speak of the 'abstract/concrete' distinction. In addition, physical objects such as chairs are regarded as clear examples of concrete things.

As we have seen, chairs are clearly not abstract. In order to count as abstract, they would have to be acausal, and they would also have to lack spatial location. Chairs fail both conditions, so they are not abstract. Since chairs are paradigms of the concrete, we should class anything that fails both conditions as concrete. But what about things that fail only one condition? Should we class them as concrete or not? In terms of Table 1, should we define 'concrete' as '(c)' or should we define it as '(a), (b), or (c)'?

This question would have little significance if categories (a) and (b) were certainly empty – but they are not. The Equator seems to be spatially located but acausal, so it seems to belong to (a). Gods and Cartesian souls are naturally seen as causally active but not spatially located, so it is tempting to classify them as (b).

Both ways of defining 'concrete' seem to have limitations. The phrase 'abstract/concrete distinction' suggests that everything is either abstract or concrete. (That is, it suggests that the distinction is exhaustive.) If we define 'concrete' as '(c)', then we will have to remember that there may be objects that

Table 1 Four sorts of object

	Not spatially located	**Spatially located**
Acausal	Abstract	(a)
Causally active	(b)	(c)

are neither abstract nor concrete – everything in (a) and (b). That will complicate our reasoning: we will not be able to infer 'x is concrete' from 'x is not abstract', nor 'x is abstract' from 'x is not concrete'. On this definition, it is misleading to speak of the 'abstract/concrete distinction': it would be clearer to speak of the 'abstract/concrete/none of the above' distinction.

Suppose instead that we define 'concrete' as '(a), (b), or (c)', which is equivalent to defining it as 'not abstract'. That definition implies that if something is not abstract, it is concrete – so, as a matter of definition, everything is either abstract or concrete. The objects in (a) and (b) are classed as concrete. The 'abstract/concrete' distinction is then an exhaustive one, so the phrase 'abstract/concrete' distinction will not mislead; and we are safe to infer 'x is concrete' from 'x is not abstract', and 'x is abstract' from 'x is not concrete'. So this way of defining 'abstract' has some advantages.

The disadvantage of this definition is that it threatens to make concreteness uninteresting. Why should this disjunctive category have any theoretical significance? It is a rag-bag into which we stuff anything that fails, for whatever reason, to be concrete, rather than a unified category which makes for genuine resemblance.

This disadvantage is not a serious problem. When we are defining a distinction, we often want it to be exhaustive. A neat way to do that is to define the second term as the negation of the first, so that the distinction is between the Fs and the non-Fs. Typically the non-Fs will have little in common other than failing to count as an F. (There are many different ways of failing to count as an event, or of failing to count as a mental state.) This is the price we pay for the benefit of having an exhaustive distinction.

Another objection to defining 'concrete' as 'not abstract' is that it privileges the abstract over the concrete. We could just as well have defined 'concrete' as 'spatially located and causally active' – that is, as '(c)' – and then defined abstract as 'not concrete'. Why start with the abstract rather than the concrete?

My impression is that starting with the abstract fits in slightly better with how philosophers have tended to use the terms. It feels somewhat revisionary to call the objects in (a) and (b), each of which is either spatially located or causally active, 'abstract'. But I don't think that much would be lost if we started with the concrete.

Perhaps we could neaten up our system of definitions by showing that categories (a) and (b) are empty (or necessarily empty). But that would be a difficult task. To pose an objection to Cartesian dualism, Kim (2001) argues that being causally active requires a spatial location. This echoes Elizabeth of Bohemia's challenge to Descartes to explain 'how the soul of a human being (it being only a thinking substance) can determine the bodily spirits, in order to bring about voluntary actions' (Shapiro 2007: 62).

In the rest of this Element, when I write 'concrete' I will mean 'not abstract'. Concrete objects are sometimes called 'concreta' (singular: 'concretum'). As well as chairs and other physical objects, plausible examples of concreta include events (e.g. the First World War) and mental state tokens (e.g. my belief that metaphysics is fascinating).

The view that there is at least one abstract object is often called 'Platonism' or 'platonism'; those who hold it, 'Platonists' or 'platonists'. 'Nominalism' is often defined as the view that there are no abstract objects; sometimes as the view that everything is concrete. Adherents of nominalism are called 'nominalists'. What those definitions mean of course depends on the meaning of 'abstract' and 'concrete'. In a debate about a particular sort of abstract object, 'platonist' and 'nominalist' can also be used to refer to those who believe, or do not believe, in the abstract objects of the sort in question. For example, one might be a nominalist about properties without being a nominalist in the first sense. In such contexts, it is convenient to call those who believe in no abstract objects whatsoever 'global nominalists'. (In the specific context of debates about properties, 'nominalist' can also mean 'someone who rejects the existence of universals'. But in this Element, I will not use the word in that sense.)

The terms 'platonist' and 'nominalist' suggest connections to ancient and medieval philosophy, respectively. They are misleading. In the sense considered here, the abstract/concrete distinction played little role in philosophy before the twentieth century (Rosen 2009: Section 'Historical Remarks'). Even a figure such as Frege, whose influence on the contemporary abstract objects debate is palpable, worked with a different group of ontological distinctions.

How does the abstract/concrete distinction relate to the modal distinction between metaphysical necessity and metaphysical contingency? It is tempting to assume that the relationship is simple: abstract objects exist necessarily, concrete objects exist contingently. That assumption fits in neatly with the appealing thought that tables are contingent existents, numbers necessary ones. But the assumption should be resisted.

The main reason for resisting it is that it is not clear that abstract objects, if they exist, exist necessarily. Often we lack evidence that an abstract object is a necessary existent. For example, one of the leading arguments for the existence of numbers rests on the idea that mathematics is indispensable to empirical science. (I will say more about this argument in the next section.) Now whether mathematics is indispensable to empirical science seems to be a contingent matter. So this argument at best gives reason to believe that numbers actually exist: it does not support the conclusion that they necessarily exist. (In other words, even if the indispensability argument succeeds, it has no implications for the modal status of the existence of numbers. To use indispensability considerations to argue that numbers exist only contingently, we would require further assumptions. See Miller 2012 for discussion.)

Moreover, we have some evidence that no abstract object exists necessarily. The evidence is simple: for each abstract object, we can imagine that object not existing. That is not conclusive or indefeasible evidence, but is evidence nonetheless. (Rosen 2002: 287–95 discusses this and other arguments for the same conclusion; see also Cowling 2017: 82–4.)

So it is not at all obvious that the abstract/concrete distinction lines up with the necessary/contingent distinction in the way suggested. If we could establish that it does, we would have an elegant theory. But until a compelling argument comes along, we should resist the assumption that there is a simple relationship between abstractness and necessity. (Sider 2013: 287 issues a similar warning.)

2.3 Who Has the Burden of Proof?

In the debate over the existence of abstract objects, who has the burden of proof? This important question is surprisingly little discussed. To find out where the burden of proof lies, we have to examine what we think of the matter before we begin to reflect on it philosophically and start to theorise about it. In other words, we need to find out what our pre-theoretical belief is.

Since the concept of an abstract object is a philosophical one, I doubt that we pre-theoretically think of things as abstract (in the sense used here). If that is right, then we do not pre-theoretically believe that there are abstract objects – and neither do we pre-theoretically believe that there are no such things.

However, there is a strong case that if there are no abstract objects, then many of our pre-theoretical beliefs are untrue. In this sense, we can be said to be committed to the existence of abstract objects.

For instance, until we start to reflect philosophically on the matter, we are happy to say that there is a prime number between four and six. Presumably, that is because we hold the belief that there is such a thing. For reasons given above, this object, if it exists, is abstract. So if there are no abstract objects then that belief is not true.

That there is a prime number between four and six is an existential belief. Not all beliefs that seem to commit us to abstract objects have that form. For example, we seem to believe that chess is a game for two players. That seems to entail that there is such a thing as chess. Very plausibly, if chess exists, it is abstract. So unless this abstract object exists, the belief is not true. In the same way, the belief that five is a prime number seems to commit us to the existence of an abstract object, the number five.

Types (if they exist) seem to be abstract objects. For instance, tokens of the word 'bread' have spatial location and causal power, but the word 'bread' itself – the type – seems to have neither. (Arguably, types are properties and their tokens are instances of them. But we do not have to take a stand on that here.) Wetzel (2009: chapter 1) argues that ordinary and scientific language abounds in apparent references to types: types of word, types of animal, types of gene, types of computer, types of atom, types of subatomic particle, and many more. Even when we are talking about a token – a particular atom or a particular move in a particular chess match – we naturally talk about a type to which it belongs (Wetzel 2009: 16–17, 21–2). This is further evidence that our pre-theoretical beliefs imply the existence of abstract objects.

Hence, it seems that our pre-theoretical beliefs depict a platonist world, not a nominalist one, and so the nominalists have the burden of proof.

However, things are more complicated. In the words of Melia (1995: 223):

> Show me a metaphysician who has tried telling a large number of people ignorant of philosophy (such as a class of first year undergraduates) that there are such things as numbers and possibilities, which we cannot see and with which we cannot interact, and I will show you a person familiar with a wide variety of incredulous stares and disbelieving sneers.

Melia's point is that platonism is implausible: when we are introduced to platonism, we do not regard it as an obvious consequence of our other beliefs, but as a striking, non-obvious thesis. Melia points out that there is 'a clash between our . . . intuitions' (Melia 1995: 223). We can state these as an inconsistent triad:

(1) Five is a prime number.
(2) If five is a prime number, then there is an abstract object.
(3) There are no abstract objects.

Pre-theoretically, we believe (1). As soon as we gain the concept of an abstract object, we find both (2) and (3) plausible. But (1), (2), and (3) cannot all be true. To portray us as pre-theoretical platonists or as pre-theoretical nominalists is therefore too simple. Although it is uncommon to put it this way, the truth is that the existence of abstract objects presents us with a paradox: we want to say that there are no such things, but our beliefs imply their existence.

If this is right, then neither side in the debate bears the burden of proof. Neither platonism nor nominalism has the advantage.

But things are even more complicated, since there is evidence that we are not committed to the literal truth of claims such as (1). Yablo (2000: 224–6; 2001: 86–7, 89–90) has pointed to a body of evidence which suggests that our attitude to claims such as (1) falls short of belief in what they literally express. Yablo argues that there are many striking similarities between mathematical language and non-literal language. I will mention just two of them.

First, both mathematical language and non-literal language turn out to enhance our expressive capacities: they help us to say things we could not otherwise say, or help us to say what we want to more quickly or effectively. To use an example of Walton's (1993: 40): describing the town of Crotone as 'on the arch of the Italian boot' specifies its location briefly and memorably. In the mathematical case, the idea is that mathematical language enables us to say things about the non-mathematical world we would otherwise find it harder or impossible to say.

Second, both types of language give rise to identity questions which are very hard to answer. For instance, saying whether the hatchet I buried yesterday is the same as the one I buried today is no easier than saying which sets the natural numbers are.

These pieces of evidence suggest that mathematical language *is* non-literal language. That may be a surprising conclusion, but in its defence Yablo (2000: 218–24; 2001: 95) argues that we sometimes speak non-literally without it being obvious to us that we're doing so.

If mathematical language is non-literal, then there is no reason to think that we regard (1) as literally true. Those who believe that there are such things as prime numbers would then have the job of convincing us that such things exist. In other words, nominalism would be the default view, and the burden of proof would be borne by platonists.

The evidence Yablo points to deserves much more discussion. At the present stage of the debate, there is no agreement over its significance. Stanley (2001: 50) claims that 'Yablo's analogies are contentious, in that many of them only someone with nominalist leanings would find compelling', though he does not argue for this claim. Alternative explanations of some of the phenomena Yablo points to are suggested by Rosen and Burgess (2005: 526–34). Moreover, Yablo's position raises a difficult question: if our attitude to the literal content of (1) is not belief, then what is it? I will return to this matter in Section 3.5.

The whole issue of burden of proof deserves much more discussion than it receives. We might easily suppose that many researchers in this area think that platonism is the default position and nominalists bear the burden of proof. I have just argued that the situation is actually more complicated.

3 For Abstract Objects

Let us now turn to arguments for the existence of abstract objects. There is no way I can do justice to all of them. I will introduce some of the most important ones in the literature and show how they are all elaborations of the same basic structure. Then I will discuss the strategies available for responding to these arguments. (Cowling 2017: chapter 1 provides a wider survey of arguments for platonism.)

I will start with the case of numbers, because no other debate offers a more developed case for platonism.

3.1 Numbers

As I have already mentioned, numbers present us with a paradox:

(1) Five is a prime number.
(2) If five is a prime number, then there is an abstract object.
(3) There are no abstract objects.

Examining the case for (3) is the task of Section 4. Let us assume for the moment that (3) has not been securely established, so that it is reasonable to reject (3). Then we have a very simple argument for platonism, made of (1) and (2):

(1) Five is a prime number.
(2) If five is a prime number, then there is an abstract object.
Therefore there is an abstract object.

This is really a telescoped version of a slightly more complex argument:

(1) Five is a prime number.
(2a) If five is a prime number, then there is a number.
(2b) If there is a number, then there is an abstract object.
Therefore there is an abstract object.

Call this the 'basic argument'. In (2), (2a), and (2b), 'If ... then' expresses the material conditional (the truth-functional conditional). The same goes for 'If ... then's in later, similar arguments. For the arguments to be valid, nothing stronger than material implication is needed.

There is obviously nothing special about (1): we can replace it with any plausible mathematical claim that seems to imply the existence of numbers, provided we adjust (2a) appropriately. For example:

Some square numbers are even.
If some square numbers are even, then there is a number.
If there is a number, then there is an abstract object.
Therefore there is an abstract object.

I will now show that some of the most important arguments for the existence of numbers have this fundamental form. They are elaborations of the following pattern, where 'X' takes the place of a sentence which seems to be true and seems to imply the existence of numbers:

(N1) X.
(N2a) If X then there is a number.
(N2b) If there is a number, then there is an abstract object.
Therefore there is an abstract object.

Call this the 'basic structure'. (In Section 3.2, I will argue that there is a more fundamental structure underlying a wide range of arguments for the existence of abstract objects.)

Let us start with the indispensability argument for the existence of numbers (and other abstract mathematical objects), because this is the argument for platonism which is currently the most discussed. The basic idea is that mathematics is indispensable to science – that is, our scientific theories would be considerably worse if they were non-mathematical – and that this establishes platonism.

Formulated in the simplest terms, the argument runs as follows:

(I1) Mathematics is indispensable to science: that is, our best scientific explanations imply the truth of some mathematical claims.
(I2) If (I1) is true, then there are abstract objects.
Therefore, there are abstract objects.

The argument is sometimes known as the '"Quine–Putnam" indispensability argument'. This title is somewhat misleading: while appealing to empirical science to establish platonism is a Quinean idea, Quine's argument for platonism involved the notion of regimentation (which I will introduce later in this section), whereas standard presentations of the indispensability argument make no mention of regimentation at all; and a case can be made that Putnam did not seek to establish the existence of abstract objects (see Liggins 2008).

The leading contemporary defender of the indispensability argument is Mark Colyvan (see Colyvan 2001, 2010).

The indispensability argument is an elaboration of the basic structure. The indispensability argument adds to the basic structure a reason for believing the instances of (N1): we should believe them because of their role in empirically confirmed scientific theories.

There are other possible justifications for the instances of (N1). For example, we might appeal not to empirical science but to mathematics itself. According to Maddy (1997: 184), 'mathematics is not answerable to any extra-mathematical tribunal and not in need of any justification beyond proof and the axiomatic method'. This view implies that we should believe claims such as (1) because mathematics tells us they are true.

Appeals to empirical science, or to formal sciences such as mathematics and mathematical logic, are called 'naturalism'. Naturalism comes in various different strengths. 'Strong' naturalism says that empirical science (or mathematics) gives philosophers an indefeasible reason to believe claims such as (1): any defeater must come from within empirical science (or mathematics), not philosophy. 'Weak' naturalism says that it gives us a reason to believe claims such as (1), but that these reasons might be overcome by philosophical argument. To make a case for platonism, we only need weak naturalism.

In setting out the indispensability argument, I deliberately left it unclear what sort of mathematical claims are involved. Does the argument concern pure mathematical claims, such as 'Five is prime', or applied ones, such as 'The mass of the Earth is 5.9736×10^{24} kg'?

In some ways, it is simpler to take the indispensability argument to concern applied mathematical claims, because these are clearly part of scientific theories. Finding the value of some quantity – the mass of the Earth, or the charge of the electron, say – can be a major scientific achievement in itself. However, this version of the argument raises the issue of how to interpret such claims. It is highly plausible that 'Five is a prime number' implies the existence of a number; it is not so obvious that 'The mass of the Earth is 5.9736×10^{24} kg' does. Perhaps it means that there is such a thing as the number 5.9736×10^{24} and that it is identical to the mass of the Earth, measured in kg, in which case it does imply the existence of a number. But perhaps it means instead that the Earth has a particular mass – one that is helpfully picked out by using the numeral '5.9736×10^{24}' even if there is no such thing as 5.9736×10^{24}. Friends of the indispensability argument need to rule out this latter interpretation.

Perhaps they are on stronger ground if they focus not on ascriptions of particular quantities, but on laws connecting them. For example, Newton's

Second Law says that the force acting on a body is the product of its mass and acceleration:

$F = ma.$

But if m and a here can be multiplied, then presumably they are numbers. They must be the values of the body's mass and acceleration on some scales of measurement – unless masses and accelerations are the sorts of things that can be multiplied.

It is more usual to present the indispensability argument as an argument for the truth of some pure mathematical claims. Pure mathematical claims are not parts of scientific theories, at least not in any everyday sense of 'part', so we cannot argue that our best scientific theories entail any pure mathematics. However, it's impossible to test a quantitative scientific theory without making pure mathematical assumptions. (Imagine trying to confirm that $F = ma$ while remaining agnostic about what results from multiplying any two numbers.) Friends of the indispensability argument claim that when a scientific theory receives empirical confirmation, the pure mathematical assumptions we need to make in order to test the theory are confirmed too.

That claim follows from the principle of 'confirmational holism': this says that when a scientific theory receives empirical confirmation, all the assumptions we need to make in order to test the theory are also confirmed. For example, suppose I have a theory about the structure of metals. This theory has implications for the density of various metals, so it can be tested by measuring the mass and volume of some metal samples, calculating their density, and comparing it with the theory's predictions. To test the theory, I need to make several mundane assumptions: for example, I have to assume that the samples really are samples of the metals in question, and I have to assume that the methods I use to measure their mass and volume are reliable. To calculate the density of each sample, I need to divide its mass by its volume, so I need to make mathematical assumptions too. (For example, if the mass is 2 kg and the volume is 0.1 m^3, then I have to assume that 2 divided by 0.1 is 20.) Confirmational holism says that if the theory is confirmed, all of these assumptions are also confirmed, including the mathematical ones.

In this way, friends of the indispensability argument call on confirmational holism and naturalism to argue for mathematical claims. They then argue that these claims imply the existence of abstract objects. Their arguments are instances of the basic structure, elaborated by appeals to holism and naturalism in support of (1).

Let us now turn to the Fregean argument for the existence of numbers. Bob Hale presents the argument as follows:

(H1) If a range of expressions function as singular terms in true statements then there are objects denoted by expressions belonging to that range

(H2) Numerals . . . do so function in many true statements (of both pure and applied mathematics)

Hence

(H3) There exist objects denoted by those numerical expressions (i.e. there are numbers). (Hale 1987: 11, numbering altered)

Hale endorses the Fregean argument. For instance, he would say that 'Five is a prime number' is true, and that 'Five' functions in that sentence as a singular term: that is to say, the word has the function of picking out a particular thing, the number five. So Hale supports (1) and (2a).

Hale (1987: 11) observes that (H3) is not yet platonism: to get from (H3) to platonism, we need to add the premiss that numbers (if they exist) are abstract objects. So he also supports (2b). Thus, Hale supports all three premises of the basic argument, and we can see that he would support many other instances of the basic structure.

The distinctive feature of Hale's approach is the way he supports premises such as (2a). Along with other Fregeans, Hale develops criteria of singular termhood: ways of showing that a particular expression functions as a singular term (see e.g. Hale 2001a, 2001b). These criteria enable Hale to defend (2a).

Fregeans focus on the semantic structure of natural language sentences such as (1). Another option at this point is to argue that the best regimentation of (1) into a formal language involves a singular term for the number five. For example, we might regiment (1) into predicate calculus as the predication 'Pf', where 'P' is a predicate expressing primeness and 'f' a singular term picking out five. We could then argue that this formula is true and requires for its truth the existence of an abstract object. Such an appeal to regimentation is part of Quine's case for the existence of abstracta (e.g. Quine 1960: 244–5, 1969: 96–100).

The Quinean appeal to regimentation bypasses some of the linguistic complexities that Fregeans have to face, because there is no claim that the regimentation has the same meaning as the sentence it regiments. But that leads us straight to the question 'What makes for a good regimentation?'. (For discussion, see Sennet and Fisher 2014.) As used here, regimentation is meant to have epistemic force, in the sense that if we regiment a sentence we take to be true, then we have some reason to believe the regimented version. (We should expect an account of regimentation to imply that it has such epistemic force.)

If regimentation is understood in this way, then the Quinean accepts instances of the basic structure, and bolsters the arguments with a rationale for premises such as (2a).

As well as defending (2a) using criteria of singular termhood, Fregeans offer a priori philosophical arguments for (1). Their starting point is 'Hume's principle':

There is a one-to-one correspondence between the *F*s and the *G*s if and only if the number of *F*s is identical to the number of *G*s.

For example, let the *F*s be some electric lamps and let the *G*s be the bulbs in these lamps. Suppose that there is a single bulb in each lamp. That is enough for there to be a one-to-one correspondence between these things. And so Hume's Principle allows us to conclude:

The number of lamps is identical to the number of bulbs.

That is a sentence that seems to imply the existence of numbers, and so can play the role of (1).

We have seen that some of the most important arguments for the existence of numbers are all elaborations of the same basic structure. This reveals some new ways of arguing for the existence of numbers. For example, one could support (1) by appeal to the role of mathematics in empirical science, and also develop criteria of singular termhood to defend (2a). That would represent a hybrid of Quinean and Fregean approaches. Or one might agree with Maddy that 'mathematics is not answerable to any extra-mathematical tribunal', thereby supporting (1) – but then regiment (1) to support (2a).

3.2 Propositions and Other Abstract Objects

Let me now introduce the standard argument for the existence of propositions. Briefly, the idea is that we need to admit the existence of propositions in order to explain the validity of some clearly valid arguments, such as these:

Bo believes that snow is white.
Mo asserts that snow is white.
Therefore, there is something that Bo believes and Mo asserts.

Mo believes that snow is white.
Jo asserts everything Mo believes.
Therefore, Jo asserts that snow is white.

According to the standard argument, we should interpret 'Bo believes that snow is white' as saying that Bo stands in the believing relation to the proposition that snow is white; and more generally, we should interpret '*X V*s that *p*' as saying that *X* stands in the *V*-ing relation to the proposition that *p*. Thus these sentences are dyadic predications. This allows us to explain the validity of the arguments by formalising them in predicate calculus as valid deductions:

Bbw
Amw
$\therefore \exists x$ (Bbx & Amx)

Bmw
$\forall x$ (Bm$x \rightarrow$ Ajx)
$\therefore$ Ajw

(see e.g. Schiffer 2003: 12–13).

Precisely how does this provide an argument for platonism? The idea is this: to explain the validity of these arguments, we should take statements of the form '*X V*s that *p*' to imply the existence of propositions; since there are true statements of that form, there are propositions; and since propositions, if they exist, are abstract objects, we reach platonism. In other words, the argument has this basic form:

(P1) Justin believes that snow is white.
(P2a) If Justin believes that snow is white, then there is a proposition.
(P2b) If there is a proposition, then there is an abstract object.
Therefore there is an abstract object.

Premiss (P2a) is supported by the observation that it helps us to explain the validity of arguments such as the examples above.

This is an example of the more general pattern of argument:

(1) *X.*
(2a) If *X* then there is an *F*.
(2b) If there is an *F*, then there is an abstract object.
Therefore there is an abstract object.

In Section 3.1, we saw that leading arguments for the existence of numbers are based on instances of this pattern. It has also been used to argue for the existence of abstract objects other than numbers or propositions. For example, we can use it to argue for the existence of properties, understood as abstract objects:

(Q1) Patience is a virtue.
(Q2a) If patience is a virtue, then there is a property.

(Q2b) If there is a property, then there is an abstract object.
Therefore there is an abstract object.

(This is essentially what Edwards 2014: 4–6 calls 'the reference argument'.) It is easy to see how arguments for the existence of other abstract objects – games, languages, concepts, theories, recipes, and so on – can be seen as instances of this basic pattern. Just replace '*X*' with a sentence that (i) seems to imply the existence of at least one of the abstract objects in question, and (ii) seems to be true.

As before, the premises of such arguments can be supported in various ways. We can recruit science to support the first premiss, thereby creating an indispensability argument. For instance, we can base an argument for the existence of properties on evolutionary biology:

(Q1*) Some traits are adaptive.
(Q2a*) If some traits are adaptive, then there is a property.
(Q2b*) If there is a property, then there is an abstract object.
Therefore there is an abstract object.

(Compare Sober 1981: Section IV.) And we can argue that psychological claims such as (P1) are part of our best scientific explanations of human behaviour (Fodor 1987).

Echoing the Fregean argument for the existence of numbers, we can argue that the word 'patience' is a singular term, thereby supporting (Q2a); or we can argue that the phrase 'that snow is white' is a singular term, thereby supporting (P2a).

A priori philosophical arguments for (1) have been offered in the case of propositions. The idea is that unless some claims such as (P1) are true, 'the concepts of rational acceptability, of assertion, of cognitive error, even of truth and falsity are called into question', so unless we uphold some ascriptions of beliefs (and other mental states), we will commit 'cognitive suicide' (Baker 1987: 134, 148).

Presented in the usual ways, arguments for platonism look very different from each other. For example, the indispensability argument for the existence of numbers, the Fregean argument for the existence of numbers, and the standard argument for the existence of propositions bear little resemblance. These differences conceal underlying similarities. We have seen that some of the most important arguments for platonism have the same basic structure, given by this pattern of argument:

(1) *X*.
(2a) If *X* then there is an *F*.

(2b) If there is an F, then there is an abstract object.
Therefore there is an abstract object.

They differ in the choices of X and F, and in how the premises are supported.

Although I have identified a pattern of deductive argument at the heart of the abstract objects debate, I am not saying that the debate proceeds only by deduction. Reasons offered for and against premises of these arguments are typically abductive. That is what we should expect, if contemporary metaphysics (and perhaps philosophy more generally) is fundamentally abductive, not deductive (Nolan 2016; Williamson 2016).

Seeing these arguments as elaborations of the basic structure just given is illuminating, not just because it sheds light on how these arguments work, but because it helps us think about how to reply to them. We can classify responses to these arguments by identifying which part of the basic structure they contest. That enables us to think about these responses in a more general way – or, if you'll excuse the pun, in a more abstract way. That is more illuminating than looking at responses to each argument one by one, because it connects together debates about different types of abstract objects. It also allows us to think about arguments not yet represented in the literature.

3.3 Responses to the Arguments: Concretism

Say that one 'resists' a premiss if one either denies it or refuses to endorse it. When presented with an argument based on the basic structure, one might resist the first premiss. Call this the 'error-theoretic' response. One might resist (2a): the 'paraphrase' response. Or one might resist (2b): the 'concretist' response. As usual, if you resist a premiss that your opponent argues for, you had better have something to say about their argument.

A nominalist is not obliged to reply to every argument for platonism in the same way. For example, they may give a paraphrase response to the standard argument for the existence of propositions but an error-theoretic response to the indispensability argument. Or a nominalist might divide up arguments for the existence of properties, taking a concretist response to some and an error-theoretic approach to others. (In fact, that is what Armstrong does, though in this section I will focus purely on the concretist part of his response.)

Let us examine the three types of response one by one, starting with the concretist response.

Concretism does not deny the existence of the objects in question. Rather, the idea is to dispute the claim that they are abstract. For example, one might concede that properties exist, but claim that they are concrete – or at least that it is unclear that they are abstract.

Armstrong's 'Aristotelian realism' about properties is an example of this strategy. According to Armstrong, each property is causally active, and it is located wherever something has it (Edwards 2014: 28–46 is a helpful guide to Armstrong's thinking on these matters). The property of being an electron is to be found just where the electrons are.

One might also accept the existence of numbers but argue that they are concrete objects. There is little plausibility to the thought that familiar concrete objects such as tables and chairs are numbers, which is probably why it receives almost no discussion. (If my chair is the number three, then why don't mathematicians show any interest in it (see Hart 1991: 91)? And is it really within my power to destroy the number three?)

If we assume that relations are concrete, a more attractive form of concretism about numbers is open to us, one that sees numbers as relations; thus the number three could be identified with the relation that every mereological sum of three *F*s bears to the property of being *F*. However, this view runs into difficulties with large infinite numbers, unless we are willing to countenance uninstantiated relations (I refer the reader to Armstrong 2004: 116–7 for the details).

The concretist strategy returns us to the arguments above (Section 2.1) about which objects should be classed as abstract. When we consider a particular object, we may well have intuitions about whether it is spatially located and whether it is causally active. For instance, numbers seem not to be spatially located or causally active; in that sense, they seem to be abstract.

Such intuitions are not sacrosanct: they can be overturned if doing so brings sufficient theoretical benefit. Perhaps regarding numbers as causally active does enough theoretical work to make up for the strangeness of the belief. But where (2b) seems to be true, it is not enough for the opponent of the argument to object that there might be a sufficient case for overturning it. One can object to any premiss of any argument merely by pointing to the epistemic possibility of a refutation of it. To cause real trouble for the argument, the opponent needs to make a good case against (2b). In other words, they need to specify what would be gained by thinking of the objects in question as concrete. The gain might be ontological simplicity (see Section 4.1). Or it might be epistemological solvency (see Section 4.2).

Where (2b) is not intuitively obvious, the argument faces a more immediate challenge. To return to an example from Section 2.1: it is just not clear whether {Edinburgh} is spatially located. If it is spatially located, it is not abstract. In a case like this, the argument has no chance of working until the platonist gives a positive case for (2b). Without such a case, their opponent is entitled to reply that we have no reason to believe this premiss of the argument.

Whether or not (2b) is intuitive, an in-depth discussion of this premiss is going to go beyond intuitions, and examine the theoretical costs and benefits of incorporating it into one's theory. One aspect of this is how well the claims made fit in with our best theories in other areas. Particularly relevant here are our general theories about what is spatially located and about what sorts of things take part in causal interactions.

3.4 Responses to the Arguments: Paraphrase

The paraphrase response is to resist (2a). The issue is what the sentences that play the role of (1) materially imply. Paraphrasers deny – or at least refuse to endorse – the claim that these sentences materially imply the existence of the objects in question. The 'refuse to endorse' version of the paraphrase response has not been popular, so I will focus entirely on the 'deny' version.

Let us return to this instance of the basic argument for the existence of numbers:

(1) Five is a prime number.
(2a) If five is a prime number, then there is a number.
(2b) If there is a number, then there is an abstract object.
Therefore there is an abstract object.

The paraphraser denies (2a). In their view, (1) does not materially imply the existence of numbers.

The obvious response is to argue that (2a) is true because (1) means what it does. This response is very plausible. 'Five is a prime number but there are no numbers' sounds self-contradictory. John Burgess (1982: 7) compares Benacerraf's claim that 'if the truth be known, there are no such things as numbers; which is not to say that there are not at least two prime numbers between 15 and 20' (Benacerraf 1965: 73) to a statement attributed to George Santayana: 'God does not exist, and Mary is His mother'. So resisting (2a) is likely to involve resisting a claim about the meaning of (1).

For example, recall the Fregean case for platonism about numbers. Fregeans not only claim that (2a) is true: they also claim that its truth flows from the meaning of (1). To back up their claims about what mathematical sentences such as (1) imply, Fregeans argue that these sentences contain singular terms for numbers. For instance, they will aim to show that the first word of (1) is a singular term for a number. This is the point of developing theories about which expressions are singular terms, and making arguments to support them.

Those who resist (2a) of the argument for numbers should have something to say about these Fregean arguments.

When they deny (2a), paraphrasers invite the following response: 'I thought that (1) means that there's an object, five, which is a prime number; and so (1) implies the existence of a number. But you deny that (1) implies the existence of a number, so you must think that (1) means something else. So what does it really mean, in your view?'.

When asked to clarify the meaning of a sentence, we commonly offer a paraphrase of it: another sentence that we take to mean the same as the original. ('What does "C'est la vie" mean?' 'It means "That's life"'.) This is the natural way to explain what (1) means, which is why this strategy for replying to the basic argument is called the 'paraphrase' response. Paraphrases are sometimes also known as 'translations', even if the original sentence and the paraphrase belong to the same language. The sort of meaning in question here is literal meaning. (Sometimes philosophers call regimentations 'paraphrases'. But this usage is potentially confusing, because a regimentation is not expected to mean the same as the original sentence (Section 3.1). I will avoid it.)

For example, the paraphraser may say: 'We misread (1) if we take it to imply the existence of a number. What it really means is the following:

(1*) It is logically necessarily that for all x, if x has the natural number structure then 'Five is a prime number' holds in x.

And (1*) can be true even if there are no numbers'.

That claim is an example of the paraphrase response known as 'modal structuralism'. The modal structuralist interprets sentences apparently about numbers as claims about what logically follows from having the natural number structure – that is, from having the structure characterised by the axioms of arithmetic. Modal structuralism is the most important paraphrase position in the philosophy of mathematics (Burgess and Rosen 1997 include a wide-ranging survey of paraphrase positions). It is usually attributed to Hellman (1989) – though that attribution is actually wrong, as we will see later in this section.

Paraphrase responses are not confined to the philosophy of mathematics. Recall the argument for the existence of properties:

(Q1) Patience is a virtue.

(Q2a) If patience is a virtue, then there is a property.

(Q2b) If there is a property, then there is an abstract object.

Therefore there is an abstract object.

One response – a currently very unpopular one – is to deny (Q2a) and claim that (Q1) simply means 'Patient people are virtuous'. So understood, (Q1) does not imply the existence of a property.

Recall also the argument for the existence of propositions:

(P1) Justin believes that snow is white.
(P2a) If Justin believes that snow is white, then there is a proposition.
(P2b) If there is a proposition, then there is an abstract object.
Therefore there is an abstract object.

One response is to claim that belief ascriptions express relations not to propositions but to sentences. This view is, naturally enough, called 'sententialism' (see e.g. Felappi 2014). For the sententialist, (P1) really means 'Justin believes "Snow is white"', so (P2a) is false: (P1) really implies the existence of a sentence, not a proposition.

When a paraphrase response is under consideration, it is common to mention a classic paper by Alston (1958). This is generally taken to contain a serious objection to the paraphrase response. But that is to misunderstand Alston's article, as I will now explain, drawing on the excellent discussion of Alston's article by Keller (2017).

The key passage of Alston's paper reads as follows:

> Here are several philosophically interesting translations . . . :
>
> 1. There is a possibility that James will come.
> 2. The statement that James will come is not certainly false.
>
> 3. There is a meaning which can be given to his remarks.
> 4. His remarks can be understood in a certain way.
>
> 5. There are many virtues which he lacks.
> 6. He might conceivably be much more virtuous than he is.
>
> 7. There are facts which render your position untenable.
> 8. Your position is untenable in the light of the evidence.
>
> Now it is puzzling to me that anyone should claim that these translations 'show that we need not assert the existence of' possibilities, meanings, virtues, and facts 'in communicating what we want to communicate'. For if the translation of (1) into (2), for example, is adequate, then they are normally used to make the same assertion. In uttering (2) we would be making the same assertion as we would make if we uttered (1), i.e., the assertion that there is a possibility that James will come. And so we would be asserting that there is a possibility (committing ourselves to the existence of a possibility) just as much by using (2) as by using (1). If, on the other hand, the translation is not adequate, it has not been shown that we can, by uttering (2),

communicate what we wanted to communicate when we uttered (1). Hence the point of the translation cannot be put in terms of some assertion or commitment from which it saves us. (Alston 1958: 9–10)

Alston points out that the relation of paraphrase is symmetrical: if sentence A means the same as sentence B, then sentence B means the same as sentence A. So if A implies the existence of Fs, then B implies the existence of Fs too. If only one of the sentences implied the existence of Fs, that would show that they did not mean the same thing after all. So either they both imply the existence of Fs, or neither of them does.

None of that is evidence against any paraphrase position. The paraphraser should claim that neither sentence implies the existence of the objects whose existence is being debated. For example, the modal structuralist should claim that neither (1) nor (1*) implies the existence of numbers. In this way, paraphrasers are perfectly capable of respecting the symmetry of the paraphrase relation.

Alston's paper poses no objection to paraphrase positions. Rather, it points out that showing that A and B are paraphrases of each other does not establish that these sentences fail to imply the existence of the objects in question. It shows that the sentences have the same ontological implications as each other, but it leaves the question of what those implications are wide open. So merely establishing that two sentences are paraphrases of each other is not enough to vindicate a paraphrase position. Showing, for instance, that (1) and (1*) mean the same is not enough to vindicate modal structuralism, for (1) and (1*) might mean the same and *both* imply the existence of numbers.

Additional argument is needed to show that neither sentence implies the existence of the objects in question – for instance, an argument against the existence of Fs, together with an argument that we should respect the apparent truth-values of the disputed sentences. That is why 'the point of the translation cannot be put in terms of some assertion or commitment from which it saves us'.

Alston's objection, then, is not an objection to paraphrase positions, but to a type of argument one might offer in their favour. Perhaps that type of argument was popular at the time when Alston was writing. In places, Quine might seem to encourage this way of arguing. For example:

Another . . . case in which a man frees himself from ontological commitments of his discourse is this: he shows how some particular use he makes of quantification, involving a prima facie commitment to certain objects, can be expanded into an idiom innocent of such commitments. . . . In this event the seemingly presupposed objects may justly be said to have been explained away as convenient fictions, manners of speaking. (Quine 1980: 103–4)

But Quine is not thinking of paraphrase positions: the paraphraser appeals to the notion of sameness of meaning – a notion which is not in good standing, according to Quine. Rather, Quine is thinking of regimentation.

Few if any contemporary paraphrasers support their view by giving arguments of the sort Alston criticised. So the value of Alston's paper is to warn us against a tempting but inconclusive line of argument. It should do nothing to lower our credence in any paraphrase position.

By the way, nothing turns on what sorts of entities *F*s are meant to be. Some philosophers have tried to 'paraphrase away' apparent reference to concrete objects such as tables, saying that 'There is a table' really means 'There are some things arranged tablewise'. Alston's paper is no threat to such positions either.

There are, however, many challenges facing the paraphraser.

It is not enough to paraphrase a few sentences that seem to imply the existence of the abstract objects in question. We want a scheme of paraphrase – that is, a recipe for generating a paraphrase of any sentence of the discourse that might play the role of (1).

A classic argument in this area illustrates the point. Suppose that 'Red is a colour' is paraphrased as 'Everything red is coloured'. Then presumably we must paraphrase 'Triangularity is a colour' as 'Everything triangular is coloured'. But that must be wrong, since even if everything triangular happened to be coloured, triangularity would still not be a colour. It is not clear to whom this argument should be attributed. Jackson (1977: 427) refers to it as a 'standard objection' and cites as an example an earlier statement by A. N. Prior. Its importance here is that it involves considering a scheme of paraphrase suggested by a paraphrase of a particular sentence. One might try to defend the original paraphrase of 'Red is a colour' as 'Everything red is coloured' by extending this to a different scheme than the one envisaged in the objection. And so the debate becomes one about schemes of paraphrase, not individual examples.

But giving a sentence-by-sentence scheme of paraphrase is not enough. As Benacerraf (1973: 666–7) points out, we need to interpret mathematical language in a way which coheres with our interpretation of non-mathematical language. One of our goals (I assume) is to find a compositional semantic theory for English, and for other natural languages: a specification of sentences' meanings based on the contributions made by their component words and phrases. From this perspective, the paraphraser owes us a compositional semantic theory for the sentences of the discourse which yields their scheme of paraphrase as a consequence. (See Dever 2008 for more on compositionality and the motivation for it.)

For an illustration of the difficulty of this, consider sentences which mix mathematical and non-mathematical language, such as:

(5) Edinburgh is large but not prime.
(6) Either three or Edinburgh is prime.
(7) There are prime numbers and tables.
(8) Bo loves Edinburgh and forty-two.

(Some would brand these sentences as unintelligible on the ground that they involve 'category mistakes'. See Magidor 2013 for counter-arguments.). I take it that 'large' is clearly a predicate (if you think it is not, swap it for your favourite example of a one-place predicate). It seems that 'large' and 'prime' play a similar semantic role in (5); we could swap them around without loss of grammaticality. The theorist who denies that 'prime' is a predicate in (1) must therefore claim that the word functions differently in (1) and (5). But this will create trouble when the theorist comes to interpret (6). How should 'prime' be interpreted here? The same way as in (5) – in which case, it functions as a predicate? Or the same way as in (1) – in which case, it does not function as a predicate? Whichever option is chosen, it seems hard for to account for the logical relations between (6) and other sentences. For instance, (6) is entailed by

(9) Three is prime.

so presumably we should interpret 'is prime' the same way in (6) and (9). But (6) is also entailed by

(10) Edinburgh is prime.

so presumably we should interpret 'is prime' the same way in (6) and (10). But that would require us to interpret the expression in the same way in (9) and (10), which is impossible if the expression is a predicate in (10) but something else in (9).

Sentences (7) and (8) raise similar problems. If 'There are tables' is an existential quantification, as it seems to be, but 'There are prime numbers' is not an existential quantification, then how are we to interpret (7)? What reading should we give to 'There are' as it appears in (7)? If 'Edinburgh' is a name but 'forty-two' is not, then how are we to read 'loves' in (8), bearing in mind that 'Bo loves Edinburgh' and 'Bo loves forty-two' collectively entail (8)?

In short, philosophers of mathematics who adopt an alternative to the default interpretation have a difficult task integrating their interpretation of mathematical sentences with their interpretation of the rest of the language. (Note that proponents of the default interpretation avoid these problems by taking mathematical language at face value.) For all I have said, perhaps a sufficiently ingenious philosopher can successfully complete the task: but the result will be a complicated semantics.

Paraphrasers often claim not just that the abstract objects in question do not exist, but that there are no abstract objects whatsoever. For example, paraphrasers in the philosophy of mathematics are often nominalists across the board. These philosophers face an additional challenge: they must show that their paraphrases are consistent with nominalism.

Modal structuralism in the philosophy of mathematics provides a good example. For the modal structuralist, true arithmetical sentences such as 'Five is a prime number' express truths about the logical consequences of having a certain structure. This raises the question: what is the metaphysics of logical consequence? Many philosophers believe that logical consequence is best understood in model-theoretic terms: for B to be a logical consequence of A is for B to come out as true on every model on which A comes out as true (Tarski 1983). This approach to logical consequence presupposes the existence of models. But models are sets. These sets are different to the example of {Edinburgh} discussed in Section 2.1, in that they do not contain physical objects at any level. They are what are called 'pure sets'. These are presumably abstract mathematical objects. So the modal structuralist who wishes to be a nominalist therefore needs either to explain how model theory does not violate nominalism, or provide an alternative nominalist account of logical consequence. They are more likely to take the latter option.

The importance of these problems should not be overstated. Every nominalist who wants to use the notion of logical consequence in their theorising needs to provide an account of logical consequence, whether or not they are a paraphraser. We will re-encounter this point in connection with Field's nominalism, which is an alternative to paraphrase nominalism (Section 3.5).

Sententialists face a similar problem. For the sententialist, belief ascriptions express relations to sentences. Some beliefs have contents that have never been tokened, so the sententialist ought to say that ascriptions of these beliefs express relations to sentence types, not sentence tokens. But sentence types, like other types, seem to be abstract objects (see Section 2.3).

The main problem for the paraphraser is making their claims about the meanings of the sentences in question plausible. Often, the sentences in question simply do not seem to mean what the paraphraser says they do. For example, 'Patience is a virtue' and 'Patient people are virtuous' seem to mean different things. (See also Field 1989: 113–5.)

Hellman's (1989) *Mathematics without Numbers* is usually regarded as the classic expression of modal structuralism. However, Hellman has claimed that paraphrase positions are

> quite implausible on linguistic grounds. Surely, ordinary mathematical
> discourse ... is not literally, *accurately rendered* ... by means of lengthy

modal conditionals concerning what would hold in arbitrary structures of the appropriate type . . . . (1998: 336)

Hellman goes on to explain that in his 1989 he was offering a 'rational reconstruction' of mathematics rather than an interpretation of mathematical language (1998: 342). So *Mathematics without Numbers* was not intended to present a paraphrase position. At the time he was writing it, Hellman rejected modal structuralism because he found its claims about linguistic meaning implausible. (More recent work, written jointly with Stewart Shapiro, indicates that Pettigrew 2008 has persuaded Hellman to change his mind on this; see Hellman and Shapiro 2019: 67–8.)

Defenders of paraphrase will probably say that these costs are worth paying. One potential benefit is especially worth mentioning. Where concretism is not a serious contender, the only options will be the paraphrase response or the error-theoretic response. In contrast to error theories, paraphrase views enable us to uphold the truth of the sentences that play the role of (1). Paraphrasers tend to regard that as one of the main benefits of their approach. In the next section, I will argue that error theories are worthy of serious attention and cannot be easily dismissed.

Another objection to paraphrasers' claims about linguistic meaning is that they violate an important methodological principle. On whether paraphrasers in the philosophy of mathematics are correct in their claims about the meaning of mathematical sentences, Burgess and Rosen write:

[T]he question seems one that it is not for us as philosophers to answer. The question of what evidence there is to favour any one hermeneutic hypothesis over any other (or over the null hypothesis that 'deep down' standard scientific language really means just about what it appears to mean 'on the surface') seems one best left to professional linguists without ulterior ontological motives. And indeed, though we find all the analyses and exegeses very implausible as accounts of the 'sense' or 'meaning' of standard language (at least in any sense or meaning of 'sense' or 'meaning' having anything to do with speakers' and writers' intentions or hearers' and readers' understandings), we are prepared to leave that issue to the linguists. (Burgess and Rosen 1997: 207)

In other words, paraphrasers are indulging in armchair linguistics: they should leave questions about the meaning of mathematical language to the experts. No doubt this argument could be extended to paraphrase responses in other domains. It threatens to show that philosophers are unjustified in believing paraphrasers' semantic claims.

Burgess and Rosen's position is arguably too extreme. One can acknowledge that work in linguistics is relevant to philosophical debates about the existence of abstract objects while denying that linguistics on its own can settle the question of what (for instance) mathematical sentences mean. Philosophers take into account pieces of evidence that play no role in linguistics: for example, the arguments for and against the existence of abstract objects. It would be irresponsible to ignore such evidence when deciding what sentences mean, because that would be to ignore some of the available evidence. (See Daly and Liggins 2011 for further discussion of philosophical deference to linguistics and other disciplines.)

However, Burgess and Rosen's comments on paraphrase do highlight a striking feature of contemporary debate over the existence of abstract objects: a lack of contact with linguistics (van Elswyk 2022 is a refreshing exception). Closer engagement promises to be fruitful, so this is an avenue for future work.

(On paraphrase responses, see von Soldokoff 2014 and Szabó 2003: section 3.)

3.5 Responses to the Arguments: Error Theory

3.5.1 Error Theories and Benacerraf's 'Mathematical Truth'

In Section 3.3, I distinguished three responses to arguments based on the basic structure: the concretist response, the paraphrase response, and the error-theoretic response. It is now time to discuss the third of these. The error theorist denies or refuses to endorse the first premiss of the argument. As before, I will focus on the 'deny' version. So the error theorist about numbers denies that five is a prime number; the error theorist about properties denies that patience is a virtue; the error theorist about propositions denies that Justin believes that snow is white. Moreover, the error theorist about numbers denies all the other claims that could be used in place of 'Five is a prime number': they deny every claim that seems to be true and seems to imply the existence of at least one number. And similarly for error theorists about other sorts of abstract object. Error theory about numbers (and other mathematical objects) is the best developed form of error theory: see Field 1989, 2016. For error theory about propositions, see Balaguer 1998a; about properties, Båve 2015. The term 'error theory' is used in different ways: as I use it here, it just expresses a claim about the truth-values of some sentences.

Consider one of the most significant and influential papers about abstract objects: Benacerraf's 'Mathematical truth' (1973). In this paper, Benacerraf proposes a dilemma for philosophers of mathematics. Either they will interpret mathematical claims as consistent with nominalism – in which case their semantic theory will be indefensible. Or they will interpret mathematical claims as concerning abstract mathematical objects – in which case they will posit abstract objects, and therefore fail to explain how we acquire mathematical knowledge. Either way, Benacerraf argues, there is a problem for the philosopher of mathematics. And it is easy to see how Benacerraf's dilemma can be extrapolated to other areas of discourse, such as property- or proposition-talk. (In the previous section, I mentioned some of Benacerraf's claims about semantics. We will touch on his claims about epistemology in Section 4.2.)

I mention this paper because it is notable that it overlooks error theory entirely. Benacerraf's argument assumes that claims such as 'Five is a prime number' are true (and are known to be true). To bypass both horns of Benacerraf's dilemma, the philosopher of mathematics can interpret mathematical language the way platonists interpret it – as concerning abstract mathematical objects – and claim that, so interpreted, sentences such as 'Five is a prime number' are not true. (Perhaps they are false, or perhaps they are neither true nor false.) In this way, the philosopher of mathematics can endorse Benacerraf's preferred semantics without claiming that there are abstract mathematical objects. So they can avoid both the semantic and the epistemological problems he raises.

This means that Benacerraf's paper should not be used to structure our thinking about the abstract objects debate. In terms of our 'basic argument', Benacerraf in effect argues that accepting (2a) and rejecting (2a) both lead to trouble. But he presupposes (1) and never discusses rejecting it.

Why does Benacerraf (1973) overlook error theory? I speculate that Benacerraf assumed that the view was not worth taking seriously. Error theories of many different discourses are often assumed to be unworthy of serious attention (Daly and Liggins 2010: 210).

3.5.2 Criticisms of Error Theories

Chris Daly and I have argued that error theories should not be dismissed: we have argued, for instance, that traditional arguments against error theory based on conservatism or Moorean considerations are unsuccessful (Daly and Liggins 2010; see also Sider 2013). These methodological arguments mean that error theories should be taken seriously.

An influential criticism of error theories is that they are uncharitable. The most promising version of this argument maintains that the error theorist is wrong to say that so many of our beliefs are untrue, because this portrays people as less rational than they really are.

There are several reasons why this criticism is not decisive. First of all, the error theorist might not be imputing untrue beliefs to anyone. All that they say is that certain sentences – those that can play the part of (1) – are not true. Whether that implies that people have untrue beliefs depends on whether anyone believes what these sentences say, literally interpreted. As we saw in Section 2.3, that is contentious. It may well be that we do not believe that five is a prime number. And if so, then denying that 'Five is a prime number' is true does nothing to impugn our rationality. One of the most famous error theorists, Field, takes this route, though this element of his thought is usually neglected:

> Fictionalism is often portrayed by platonists as a radical position, quite at odds with the views of the average non-philosopher. I rather doubt that this is so. I don't think it at all obvious that the average person … literally believes that there are mathematical entities. The average non-philosopher, I suspect, has not thought enough about what platonism involves and what fictionalism involves to have anything like a consistent view of the matter. (Field 1989: 8; see also Field 2016: P-3)

In many cases, though, it will be plausible to claim that we have the beliefs in question. Even so, that need not be problematic, provided the error theorist can explain how we came to form them in a way that does not imply that we are less rational than we really are. In other words, the error theorist needs to give these beliefs some positive epistemic status. (What precisely 'positive epistemic status' might be here is a delicate epistemological question: see Kovacs 2021: Section 2 for relevant discussion.)

The details of how to do this will vary from case to case. One option for the error theorist is to appeal to the role of testimony (Liggins 2020: 86–7). The idea is this. Lots of our beliefs come from what our parents and teachers taught us. We had no reason to doubt what they said, so it was not irrational of us to form these beliefs. The reasons to doubt are philosophical arguments, such as the ones we will discuss in Section 4; someone who is unaware of these arguments' existence – and ill-equipped to evaluate their cogency – cannot be faulted for failing to take them into account.

Another type of response is to give the beliefs a positive epistemic status by associating them with truths. There are several versions of this. Perhaps we confuse the untrue belief with the true one (see Markosian 2004: 69–73 for a version of this move in the philosophy of time). Or perhaps holding the untrue belief helps us to communicate the true one (we will see in Section 3.5.5 that this strategy is popular with contemporary nominalists in the philosophy of mathematics). Or perhaps the untrue belief is, to use Sider's term, 'quasi-true'. A belief B that implies the existence of Fs is quasi-true iff there is some truth C such that, had there been Fs, C would have been true and it would have metaphysically necessitated the truth of B (Sider 1999: 340); this is meant to capture the idea that B is true apart from presupposing the existence of Fs.

So when the error theorist is charged with being uncharitable, there is a range of responses available to them.

Opponents of error theory may well appeal to the reasons they have for believing (1). So I will now review some of those reasons and indicate what the error theorist may say in reply.

As I mentioned in Section 3.2, Baker suggests that to deny every ascription of mental states such as belief would amount to 'cognitive suicide'; for instance, she argues that it is unclear how there could be assertion unless there are some true ascriptions of belief (1987: 138–42). In response, Andrew Cling has argued that these considerations assume what they set out to prove, and are best regarded as a challenge to Baker's opponents to develop their own rival accounts of phenomena such as assertion (Cling 1989; see also Daly 2013).

We saw in Section 3.1 that Fregeans offer a priori philosophical arguments for (1), based on Hume's Principle:

There is a one-to-one correspondence between the Fs and the Gs if and only if the number of Fs is identical to the number of Gs.

In reply, nominalists question Hume's Principle, and allege that it has been confused with the following, more plausible principle:

If there are numbers, then: there is a one-to-one correspondence between the Fs and the Gs if and only if the number of Fs is identical to the number of Gs.

(Field 1984). Unlike Hume's Principle, this conditional principle cannot be used to argue for the existence of numbers.

In Section 3.1, I distinguished two types of naturalism. Weak naturalism says that empirical science (or mathematics) gives us a reason to believe claims such as (1), but that these reasons might be defeated by philosophical argument. Strong naturalism says that it gives us indefeasible reason which cannot be so defeated.

Error theorists are likely to concede that weak naturalism is highly plausible, and argue that the reasons empirical science (or mathematics) gives for believing claims such as (1) are outweighed by other evidence. (In Section 4, I will examine the case against the existence of abstract objects.) What should error theorists say in response to arguments for (1) based on strong naturalism?

The first thing they should say is that strong naturalism is not obviously true. Any appeal strong naturalism has is likely to stem from confusing it with weak naturalism. Where arguments for strong naturalism are given, they tend to draw on the historic track of science compared with the historic track record of philosophy. Lewis's 'Credo' is a good example:

> Mathematics is an established, going concern. Philosophy is as shaky as can be. To reject mathematics for philosophical reasons would be absurd . . . Even if we reject mathematics gently – explaining how it can be a most useful fiction, 'good without being true' – we still reject it, and that's still absurd.

(Lewis 1991: 58. After the words 'good without being true' Lewis footnotes Field's *Science without Numbers*.)

Lewis's approach has been influential (see the references given at Daly and Liggins 2011: 323). However, it has also met with considerable resistance.

In the present context, perhaps the most fundamental response focuses on what it is to be an 'established, going concern'. Error theorists should acknowledge that mathematics is an established discipline with a solid track record of producing theories that are excellent by mathematical standards. But they should also question whether that means that we should think that these theories are true. The relation between mathematical excellence and truth seems to be a philosophical matter – one that can't be resolved simply by appeal to mathematics, or to the historic track records of philosophy and mathematics (see Balaguer 2009: 153–7). The same points apply to appeals to science to establish claims such as (1). (For discussion of Lewis's Credo, see Paseau 2005 and Daly and Liggins 2011: section 3. For relevant discussion of philosophy's historic track record, see Stoljar 2017.)

The strong naturalist says that some disciplines provide philosophically indefeasible reasons for belief. They need to explain why they think these particular disciplines have this privileged status. Perhaps 'mathematics is not answerable to any extra-mathematical tribunal' (Maddy 1997: 184), but astrology certainly is answerable to non-astrological tribunals. What explains why mathematics has authority but astrology does not? This is what Rosen (1999: 471) calls the 'authority problem'. The problem cannot just be solved by appealing to the internal standards of the discipline in question: mathematicians produce work that is excellent by the internal standards of mathematics, but astrologers may well produce work that is excellent by astrological standards too (Rosen 1999: 471–2). A strong naturalist might try to explain the authority of science by pointing to its empirical success; or they might explain the authority of mathematics by pointing to its role in empirically successful science. These lines of thought point towards the indispensability argument.

3.5.3 Error-Theoretic Responses to the Indispensability Argument

Since the indispensability argument has such importance to contemporary debate over the existence of abstract objects, I will discuss error-theoretic responses to it in particular detail.

In Section 3.1, I distinguished different versions of the indispensability argument. One focuses on applied mathematical claims, such as 'The mass of the Earth is 5.9736×10^{24} kg', that are parts of well-confirmed scientific theories. The other focuses on pure mathematical claims, such as 'Five is prime'. The latter argument rests on confirmational holism; the former does not.

One way of attacking the 'pure' version of the indispensability argument is to attack confirmational holism. Is it really true that confirming a theory also confirms all the assumptions we have to make in order to test it? Joe Morrison (2010, 2012) argues that the confirmational holism relied on by the indispensability argument has never received serious argumentative support; he suggests that it is popular only because philosophers have confused it with other, better-supported holistic claims about evidence (see also Field 2016: P-31).

Even worse for the defender of this form of the indispensability argument, there is mounting evidence against confirmational holism. Elliott Sober argues that appeals to confirmational holism can violate a well-established principle of confirmation, namely, the principle that an observation can confirm a theory without confirming all of its logical consequences. This example illustrates the point:

> I draw a card at random from a standard deck of cards without looking at it. The probability that it is the seven of hearts is 1/52. You then inform me that the card is red. This information confirms the hypothesis that the card is the seven of hearts ... in the sense of making the hypothesis more plausible than it was before; the probability that I have the seven of hearts has just increased to 1/26. However, this information does not confirm the hypothesis that the card I hold is a seven; the probability that I have a seven remains what it was, namely 1/13. (Sober 2000: 264)

Hence for Sober '[t]he confirmation relation that confirmational holism invokes is *bizarre*' (2000: 264). And Maddy provides evidence against confirmational holism drawn from scientific practice: scientists frequently use idealisations that they know to be false, such as the assumption that projectiles face no air resistance (Maddy 1997: 143–94; 2005: 454–5; only in the latter is Maddy explicit that confirmational holism is the culprit).

So the 'pure' version of the indispensability argument faces a serious challenge because it relies on confirmational holism. However, this does not get to the heart of the matter, because the 'applied' version of the indispensability argument does not rely on holism. How should an error theorist reply to the 'applied' version?

Colyvan (2010: 286–7) draws a valuable distinction between 'easy road' and 'hard road' responses to the indispensability argument. According to the hard road response, well-confirmed scientific theories which entail the existence of abstract objects can all be replaced with new theories that are consistent with nominalism – so mathematics is not indispensable to science after all. In contrast, the nominalist who takes the easy road concedes that mathematics is indispensable to science, but maintains that the indispensability argument fails to establish platonism.

Although Colyvan draws this distinction within the debate over the metaphysics of mathematics, the same distinction can be applied to any indispensability argument. For example, if we argue that properties exist on the grounds that evolutionary theory entails their existence, an opponent might offer a new version of evolutionary theory that is consistent with nominalism. That would be a 'hard road' response.

3.5.4 Hard Road Responses

Hard road responses in any area face a formidable technical programme: they need to establish where our best scientific theories entail the existence of the abstract objects in question, and then supply alternative theories which avoid that entailment. Unlike the 'paraphrase' strategy considered earlier, the hard road theorist does not claim that the alternatives pick out more clearly what the original theories said all along. On the contrary: because the original theories entail platonism, but the replacements do not, they must differ in meaning. Let us call theories that are consistent with nominalism 'nominalistic', all others 'platonistic'. In these terms, the hard road nominalist takes a platonistic theory and offers a nominalistic alternative.

The replacement theories have to be just as theoretically virtuous as the original theories. Replacing a good platonistic theory with a worse nominalistic one would not show that platonistic assumptions are dispensable! (See Colyvan 2001: 76–81.) Interestingly, Field (2016: chapter 5; 1989: 18–19, 192–3) suggests that because his nominalistic replacements do not invoke causally irrelevant abstract objects, they might be more explanatory than the original platonistic theories. If genuine, this benefit presumably carries over to nominalisation programmes in other areas.

Field's strategy was to offer a way of nominalising field theories in flat space-time, thereby giving a way to nominalise Newtonian gravitational theory and other theories of this type. Of course, Newtonian gravitational theory is no longer one of our best theories – space-time is now known to be curved – but Field's idea was that this technical work makes it plausible that our current best theories can be given nominalistic replacements that are equally good, if not better.

Field's programme of nominalising science dominated discussions of nominalism in the 1980s and 1990s. In the course of the debate, Field's response to the indispensability argument met with many objections. This is not the place to summarise them all: I will just mention three of the most important ones.

(MacBride 1999 and Leng 2010: Section 3.2 survey the debate over Fieldian nominalism.)

First of all, there is the objection that the methods Field developed do not carry over to other areas of science – in particular, those, such as quantum theory, that use 'phase spaces'. (The classic expression of this is David Malament's review of *Science without Numbers* (Malament 1982); see also Balaguer 1998b: chapter 6 and Lyon and Colyvan 2008.) Applying Field's methods to these theories seems to require the existence of such things as possibilities, but it is far from clear that these are concrete objects.

Field's reformulations of physical theory assume the existence of space-time points: entities with zero volume, each of which exists for just an instant, that collectively constitute space-time. The second objection is that the nominalist is not allowed to posit such things. In particular, any worries that arise about epistemic access to abstract mathematical objects (to be discussed in Section 4.2) seem to apply equally to space-time points. In response, Field (1989: 69–73) argues that he is free to posit space-time points because they stand in spatio-temporal relations to human beings and are causally active.

The third objection concerns metalogic. Field makes use of the concept of logical consequence, but can he account for this without positing mathematical objects? As we saw when discussing modal structuralism (Section 3.4), many philosophers understand logical consequence in terms of models, which are sets. Field does not adopt this account: instead, he attacks it, and proposes that logical consistency be treated as a primitive notion (1989: 30–8).

All three objections concern the resources – the entities and concepts – available to Field. They can be seen as facets of a more general objection, that Field uses resources that are inconsistent with his nominalism, or with his motivation for nominalism about mathematical objects.

'Hard road' responses to other indispensability arguments face similar objections. Consider the indispensability argument for properties, which says that claims such as

(Q1*) Some traits are adaptive.

appear in scientific theories that merit our belief; since traits are properties, we should believe in properties. One response to this is to replace theories mentioning traits with theories that use higher-order resources. Thus (Q1*) would be replaced with:

$\exists X \, AX.$

(see Liggins 2021: section 3.2). Here '*X*' is a variable holding the syntactic position of a predicate, bound by the higher-order existential quantifier '∃'; and '**A**' is a predicate of predicates. But these resources raise suspicions: are they really intelligible? And, if they are, is a nominalist entitled to use them – or is quantification into predicate position just quantification over sets or other abstract entities (Quine 1970: 68)? Quantification into sentence position is a device that might be used to help avoid quantification over propositions: for instance, one might replace 'Peter believes some proposition' with:

∃*p* B*p*.

where '*p*' is a variable in sentence position and 'B' is an operator meaning 'Peter believes that'. It raises similar questions – most importantly, are formulae that use it just disguised quantification over propositions or other abstract objects? Admitting quantifiers into predicate and sentence position as legitimate resources, irreducible to first-order quantification, is leading to exciting theoretical developments (see Skiba 2021 for a survey and references).

   Another way to avoid quantification over propositions would be to take a leaf out of the sententialists' book, by talking about sentences instead of propositions. (Unlike the sententialist, the error theorist would maintain that these are new and better explanations, not restatements of the old ones.) But since some beliefs have contents that have never been tokened, a version of the problem mentioned in Section 3.4 appears here: the new explanations must talk about sentence types, not sentence tokens – but sentence types appear to be abstract objects.

   In 1998, Field commented wryly: 'Unfortunately, the nominalization project is nontrivial. I did a certain amount of work trying to carry it out some time ago. I won few converts, but I'm a stubborn kind of fellow who is unwilling to admit defeat' (Field 1998: 400, footnote removed). Field has begun to sound sympathetic to the easy road response to the indispensability argument for mathematical objects (see Field 2016: P-30–P-37).

3.5.5 Easy Road Responses

Having considered hard road responses to indispensability arguments, let us now consider easy road ones. I will focus on the mathematical case, since this is where the debate is most developed. (See Balaguer 1998a for an easy road approach to proposition-talk.)

   For those who take the easy road, our best scientific theories imply the existence of the objects in question, and they cannot be replaced with equally good ones that do not – but still this fails to show that the objects exist.

According to the most promising versions of the easy road, the reason it fails to show this is that speaking in terms of the objects in question brings expressive benefits: it helps us to say more or to say things in a more useful way. As Balaguer (1998b: 141) puts it: 'the nominalistic content of empirical science is its picture of the physical world, whereas its platonistic content is the canvas . . . on which this picture is painted'. So mathematics is indispensable to science, even though science has not discovered that mathematical objects exist. The claim is that mathematics is useful in science because it helps us make claims about concrete objects which it would otherwise be more difficult to make, or perhaps impossible. I like to call this claim 'abstract expressionism'. (Easy road responses to the indispensability argument include: Balaguer 1998b: chapters 5 and 7; Melia 1995, 2000; Yablo 2000, 2001, 2002; Leng 2010.)

Why might abstract expressionism be true? It may be because mathematical language provides a systematic way of ascribing particular lengths, masses and so on. If we had a different predicate for each length, we would have to learn infinitely many predicates in order to master length-talk. Bringing in mathematics – 'is 1 m long', 'is 2 m long', 'is 3 m long' and so on – provides us with a systematic way of ascribing lengths. Moreover, some facts about lengths are reflected in this way of picking them out: to give one example out of very many, anything that is 1m long is shorter than something that is 2 m long, just as (according to mathematics) 1 is less than 2. These structural similarities between numbers and physical magnitudes make it convenient to use mathematical language when ascribing these magnitudes (see e.g. Balaguer 1998b: 138; Melia 1998: 70–1). And even where nominalistic alternatives to platonistic scientific theories are available, they are less useful to work with: platonistic versions are more suggestive and easier to compare with alternatives (Yablo 2000: Section 13). It is easy to imagine similar claims in other areas: for example, using the predicates 'believes that it will snow' and 'hopes that it will snow' brings out that both the belief and the hope have the same content, in a way that using two unconnected predicates would not. This is more convenient and more systematic.

In the philosophy of mathematics, the most important response to the easy road is to argue that mathematics has a greater role in science than abstract expressionism allows. According to this line of argument, mathematics plays a genuinely explanatory role in science, or at least in some parts of science. To establish this, philosophers have offered examples of scientific explanations in which mathematics plays a genuinely explanatory role, not a merely expressive one (see e.g. Lyon and Colyvan 2008). The example that has received most discussion is due to Alan Baker (2005), and it concerns periodical cicadas. Three species of this insect have life-cycles of either thirteen or seventeen years.

Why are their life-cycles a prime number of years long? Baker argues that the mathematical properties of prime numbers are part of the reason why: having a life cycle whose length in years is a prime number brings evolutionary advantages. Baker's critics have maintained that mathematics plays an expressive rather than an explanatory role in explaining the length of the life-cycles: it helps us to represent periods of time and the relations between them (see e.g. Leng 2010: 244–9).

This debate has bogged down in clashing intuitions and contentious questions about the burden of proof (Knowles and Liggins 2015: 3403–4). Perhaps part of the problem is that the distinction between explanatory role and expressive role has not been picked out sharply enough. Doing so would help to advance the debate. (For relevant discussion, see Lyon 2012 and Saatsi 2016.)

How exactly does bringing in abstract objects help us to talk about concrete ones? Abstract expressionists owe us an answer to this question.

The leading answer in the literature is Yablo's: mathematical talk is figurative language, and figurative language is to be accounted for using Kendall Walton's notion of 'prop-oriented make believe' (Walton 1993; see Yablo 1998: 250–1; 2001, 2002, 2005). The crucial idea here is that what is true within a game of make-believe can depend on what is actually the case, and so utterances that are true within a game can convey information about how things really are.

Yablo does not claim that we actually make believe when we use mathematical language: rather, his view is that we engage in 'simulated belief'. How does this differ from make-believe? According to Yablo: 'Making believe is an amalgam of (i) being as if you believe, and (ii) being that way through your deliberate efforts' whereas simulated belief involves only (i) (2001: 90; see also 97–9). He explains:

> Someone is simulating belief that S if although things are in relevant respects as if they believed that S, when they reflect on the matter they find that they do not believe it; or at least are agnostic on the matter; or at least do not feel the propriety of their stance to depend on their belief that S if they have one. They do not believe that S except possibly per accidens. (2001: 90)

Yablo's examples of simulated belief include that of a film-goer simulating belief that she is being attacked by a giant squid.

Arguably, Yablo's position lacks psychological plausibility. Stanley (2001: 47–9) raises an ingenious psychological objection concerning autism. Briefly: if mathematical language is figurative and forms part of a make-believe game, then we should expect people with autism to find it difficult to take part in mathematical discourse; but that is not the case, so Yablo's view stands refuted. (For Yablo's responses, see Yablo 2001: 90–1, 97–9; Liggins 2010b discusses Stanley's objection in detail.)

Even if Stanley's argument fails, Yablo's explanation of how mathematical language expands our expressive capacities faces a simpler psychological objection: it just does not seem as though we are simulating belief. It seems that Yablo has no prospect of an explanation of why we take ourselves not to be simulating belief. (See Liggins 2014: 608–10.)

In more recent work, Yablo offers a different explanation, based around the notion of 'subject matter' (e.g. Yablo 2014), work that is too rich to be summarised here. It deserves close examination, partly because of its intrinsic interest, and partly because if it works in the case of mathematical language it probably works in a wide variety of other cases.

'Mathematical surrealism' is the name of more recent challenge to abstract expressionism. It is the view that abstract expressionist accounts of mathematics can be used to generate a hard road response – and that this response is better. The idea is that, when provided with a well-confirmed platonistic scientific theory, we can always prefix the theory with a suitable operator, and the result is a 'parasitic alternative' (Boyce 2020: 2816) that is nominalistic and just as virtuous as the original theory in other respects. The content of the operator is drawn from abstract expressionist thinking; there are various possibilities. The prefix might be:

The following claim is nominalistically adequate: . . .

Or if the platonistic scientific theory presupposes a mathematical theory M, then the prefix might be:

If M were true and the concrete realm were just as it in fact is, then it would be the case that . . .

or

Necessarily, if M is true and the concrete realm is just as it in fact is, then . . .

(see Boyce 2020: 2817 and works cited therein). If all our well-confirmed platonistic scientific theories can be turned into nominalistic ones in this way, with no loss of theoretical virtue, then we have a successful hard road response to the indispensability argument, because we have shown how to make our best theories nominalistic.

Mathematical surrealism is an ingenious idea, but it faces two difficult questions.

First: what reason do we have to think that the new theory is as virtuous as the platonistic one? There is no particular reason to think that a theory retains all its virtues when prefixed with an operator such as 'Necessarily, if M is true and the concrete realm is just as it in fact is, then . . . ' (see Dorr 2010; Boyce 2020: 2825–8 for relevant discussion).

Second: why should we think the hard road response that uses the replacement theory is better than an easy road response? For Boyce, an important difference is that the easy road requires one to reject inference to the best explanation as invalid, whereas the hard road does not (2020: 2817, 2822). But it is far from clear that the easy road really does require the rejection of inference to the best explanation. I suggest that the notion of expressive benefit is important here. Melia (1995: 227–9) argues that it is irrational to infer to the best explanation we can express, when we have reason to think that there is a better explanation we cannot express. So, arguably, Melia upholds the validity of inference to the best explanation while warning that its application should not be distorted by what we happen to be able to express: our expressive capacities ought not to shape our inferential behaviour in that way. Perhaps Boyce would be on firmer ground if there were consensus on how best to articulate inference to the best explanation. But in fact there are numerous competing versions (see McCain and Poston 2017). That makes it harder to show that Melia's approach requires inference to the best explanation to be rejected.

The debate between abstract expressionists and surrealists is an in-house debate between nominalists. Should surrealism prevail, abstract expressionists might not be terribly disappointed, if their ultimate goal is to defend nominalism.

Error-theoretic responses to arguments for the existence of abstract objects meet a weighty challenge from indispensability arguments. But we have seen that there is a variety of responses error theorists can make. They have plenty of work to do dealing with phase spaces, cicadas, surrealists, and giant squid.

4 Against Abstract Objects

We have seen that Quine argued for the existence of abstract objects. In earlier work, he and Goodman claimed that there are no abstract objects. 'Why do we refuse to admit the abstract objects that mathematics needs? Fundamentally this refusal is based on a philosophical intuition that cannot be justified by appeal to anything more ultimate' (Goodman and Quine 1947: 105).

This statement is admirably candid, but it lacks persuasive force. Nominalists must have more to say about why we should be nominalists. (In fairness, I should mention that Quine and Goodman go on to give other reasons for embracing nominalism.) In this section I introduce two motivations for nominalism, and set out some of the complexities they raise. As we will see, neither is best understood as a self-standing argument for nominalism. It is better to regard them as challenges to platonism.

4.1 Ontological Motivations for Nominalism

Simplicity is also known as 'parsimony' or 'economy', and it comes in several varieties. The sort that is relevant here is ontological simplicity. It seems that the nominalist has a simpler ontology than the platonist, because the platonist posits abstract objects whereas the nominalist does not.

But simplicity is more complicated than that. Lewis (1973: 87) distinguishes different sorts of ontological simplicity. A theory is 'quantitatively' simple if it posits fewer entities; it is 'qualitatively' simple if it posits fewer types of entities.

It is impossible to judge the quantitative simplicity of a theory without knowing its details, but it is fair to say nominalist theories tend to be quantitatively simple compared with platonist ones. Most platonist accounts of properties, propositions, and mathematical entities posit infinitely many abstract objects. Mathematics teaches us that some infinite numbers are greater than others, but set theory posits so many objects that mathematics lacks a number to count them.

However, it is controversial whether quantitative simplicity is a theoretical virtue. Lewis (1973: 87) denied that it is (see Nolan 1997 for discussion). Some would also deny that qualitative simplicity is a virtue (see e.g. Huemer 2009), but, like many metaphysicians, I will assume that it is, and examine the significance of qualitative simplicity to the abstract objects debate.

Let 'global' nominalism be the claim that there are no abstract objects whatsoever. And let 'nominalism about *F*s' be the claim that there are no abstract objects that are *F*s. For example, a nominalist about properties claims that either there are no properties or they are concrete objects. A nominalist about properties need not be a global nominalist: they might think there are some abstract objects that are not properties (propositions, perhaps).

Nominalism about a specific kind of abstract object that falls short of global nominalism is hard to defend by appeal to simplicity. This nominalist does posit abstract objects of one sort, so it is hard to see their theory as qualitatively simple compared with other platonist theories. Moreover, such a position faces challenges over its motivation. For instance, consider the view that there are no abstract mathematical objects, but there are propositions, and these are abstract objects. Anyone who holds this view faces the challenge: why do your reasons for avoiding abstract mathematical objects not carry over to propositions? If that avoidance is motivated by epistemological considerations (see Section 4.2) then why do those considerations not apply to propositions as well? It may be possible to overcome such challenges, but they certainly give the non-global nominalist more work to do.

Let us turn now to global nominalism. It seems that any form of global nominalism is bound to be qualitatively simpler than a theory that posits both abstract and concrete objects: the latter posits objects of both those types, the former only posits concrete objects. An under-discussed option for platonists here is to deny the existence of concrete objects, and say that abstract objects give rise to the perceptual experiences that convince us concrete objects exist (see Szabó 2003: 29).

So far I have assumed that when we assess qualitative simplicity, it is appropriate to take 'abstract object' and 'concrete object' as kinds. Actually, that is not so clear. There is a wider methodological problem concerning what to count as a kind when judging the qualitative simplicity of a theory. At one extreme, for each object o posited by the theory, we could take 'thing that is identical to o' as a kind: then there would be as many kinds as objects posited. At the other extreme, we could say that the only thing to count as a kind is 'self-identical object': then each theory that posits at least one thing would posit just one kind. In between these extremes there are many different alternatives. Our evaluation of a theory depends on what we count as a kind, but which alternative should we pick, and why? (See Oliver 1996: 7. Lewis 1973: 87 speaks of 'fundamentally different kinds of entity', which may help, but does not completely resolve the problem.)

Rather than pressing this problem, platonists are more likely to point out that appeals to simplicity are inconclusive. Nominalist theories may have the virtue of simplicity, but that is just one virtue among many: their simplicity and other virtues may well be outweighed by their theoretical vices. A well-known formulation of Occam's Razor states that 'Entities are not to be multiplied without necessity'. The last two words are important here: although a shortage of simplicity may well count against platonist theories, we cannot establish nominalism merely on the basis of simplicity. Rather, we have to compare the overall theoretical benefit of positing abstract objects with the overall theoretical benefit of not. So the appeal to simplicity advances debate by issuing a challenge to platonists. Whether it motivates nominalism depends on whether platonists can meet the challenge. Abstract objects might be complications we cannot do without.

Because explanatory power is an important theoretical virtue, one way for platonists to meet the challenge is to show that we need abstract objects to explain the phenomena that need explaining. So considerations of simplicity lead us back to indispensability arguments (see Sections 3.1 and 3.2).

4.2 Epistemological Motivations for Nominalism

Epistemological motivations for nominalism are developed in most depth in the debate over the existence of abstract mathematical objects, so I will focus on that debate. Much of it carries over straightforwardly to nominalism about other sorts of abstract objects. (On epistemic challenges to belief in properties, see Swoyer 1996.)

We saw in Section 3.5 that Benacerraf (1973) posed a dilemma for all philosophers of mathematics. Part of this was to argue that if we take mathematical claims to be accurate descriptions of abstract mathematical objects, then we will be unable to explain how people acquire mathematical knowledge. For example, '2+2=4' will be interpreted as a claim about two abstract objects, the number two and the number four – but because these objects are abstract, we are unable to know how they are related, so the platonist is at a loss to explain how we come to know that 2+2=4.

Benacerraf's argument assumes that the platonist will not want to deny that people have such knowledge. This assumption is reasonable. Since it forms part of a dilemma, Benacerraf does not endorse this argument: he simply adds it to the discussion. It potentially generalises to other platonist theories. For example, many want to say that we know that the proposition *Fido barks* entails the proposition *something barks*: but if propositions are abstract objects, that makes it impossible to explain how we gain this knowledge.

Benacerraf's argument uses a non-obvious epistemological assumption: it relies on the claim that we know about objects only if we are causally related to them. Benacerraf (1973: 671) justifies it by appealing to causal theories of knowledge, which were popular at the time.

According to Lewis (1986: 109), Benacerraf's whole strategy is flawed, because there is no way of using an epistemological assumption to refute platonism: 'Our knowledge of mathematics ... is ever so much more secure than our knowledge of the epistemology that seeks to cast doubt on mathematics. ... Causal accounts of knowledge are all very well in their place, but if they are put forward as *general* theories, then mathematics refutes them'. Perhaps Lewis is alluding here to the fact that causal theories were not always intended as general theories (for instance, Goldman (1967: 357) says he intends to account only for knowledge of 'empirical propositions'). Lewis's argument presupposes that we begin philosophical reflection knowing some truths about abstract objects. But in Section 2.3 I cast doubt on that assumption. If nominalists have the burden of proof, then perhaps Lewis is right; but if they do not, it is hard to see how our knowledge of mathematics can have the force Lewis takes it to have.

Causal theories of knowledge have not worn well. Contemporary epistemologists reject them for reasons that have nothing to do with abstract objects (see

Swain 1998). So Benacerraf's argument has few, if any, adherents nowadays. Yet the sense remains that abstract objects raise an epistemological problem.

Field (1989: 25–30, 68, 230–9; 2016: section 5) offers a different way of articulating this problem. Unlike Benacerraf's argument, Field's does not rely on any assumptions about necessary conditions on knowledge (Field 1989: 232–3). It is epistemological only in the broad sense of concerning true belief.

Field's argument centres on the mathematical beliefs held by mathematicians. As an error theorist, Field thinks that these are largely untrue, because the objects that are required for their truth do not exist. He points out that platonists will accept that most of the mathematical beliefs held by mathematicians are true; they will think that, although mathematicians make the occasional mathematical mistake, their mathematical beliefs are largely accurate. This phenomenon would be 'so striking as to demand explanation' (1989: 26); the problem for the platonist is about how they can explain it.

There are two strategies open to them, Field argues. They can give a causal explanation – but the acausal nature of the entities they posit rules this out. Or they can give a non-causal explanation – but for Field

> it is very hard to see what this supposed non-causal explanation could be. Recall that on the usual platonist picture, mathematical objects are supposed to be mind- and language-independent; they are supposed to bear no spatio-temporal relations to anything, etc. The problem is that the claims the platonist makes about mathematical entities appear to rule out any reasonable strategy for explaining the systematic correlation in question. (1989: 231)

So it seems that the platonist can give no explanation of mathematicians' mathematical accuracy. In other cases of non-accidentally true belief, it is possible to give an explanation: for instance, we do not know all the details, but we have the makings of a scientific account of how our perceptual faculties provide us with true beliefs about our environment. Field's point is that it is hard to imagine what shape a convincing platonist explanation of mathematicians' mathematical accuracy would take.

Contemporary mathematical theories have an axiomatic structure: mathematicians' mathematical beliefs are deduced from the axioms of the area of mathematics in question. Since true axioms only have truths as logical consequences, explaining why mathematicians' beliefs in their axioms tend to be true would go a long way towards explaining mathematicians' mathematical accuracy, as Field (1989: 231–2) acknowledges. But it is hard to see what form a satisfactory explanation could take – or so Field claims.

At this point, exposition of Field is complicated by the fact that that different groups of philosophers interpret his argument in different ways. Sjölin Wirling (forthcoming) calls the two camps 'Team Explanatory Power' and 'Team

Undercutting Defeat'. The dispute is about what we should conclude from being unable to envisage a satisfactory platonist explanation of mathematicians' mathematical accuracy.

According to Team Explanatory Power, the significance of this is that we should lower our credence in platonism. Platonist accounts of mathematics fail to explain a phenomenon they ought to explain, and that counts against them. Team Undercutting Defeat, on the other hand, take the significance to be that it removes the justification for mathematicians' mathematical beliefs (see e.g. Clarke-Doane 2017).

Here, I will avoid the debate over what Field really intended, and focus on my preferred interpretation, that of Team Explanatory Power, because I think this argument offers a more promising case for nominalism.

I say 'promising' rather than 'successful', because it is important to appreciate the dialectical status of Field's contribution. If we treat it as an attempt to refute platonism about mathematical objects, then I think it has little prospect of succeeding. The weak spot is the passage quoted above: 'it is very hard to see what this supposed non-causal explanation could be'. Here Field suggests that it will not be possible for the platonist to give a convincing non-causal explanation of the phenomenon in question, but he does not provide a strong reason for thinking so, merely that it doesn't seem to him that this is possible. Considered as an objection to platonism, this is flimsy (see Liggins 2010a: 74).

When he introduces his argument, Field (1989: 25) uses the word 'challenge', and that seems a better way of understanding its significance. At the moment, platonist theories do not explain why mathematicians' mathematical beliefs are accurate. That counts against them. But we cannot rule out that a sufficiently ingenious platonist will be able to explain the phenomenon.

Field's argument involves the idea that it is a theoretical cost to leave some phenomena unexplained – they 'call for explanation'. This methodologically important idea is poorly understood, as Dan Baras has emphasised; his 2022 is a book-length discussion of the notion. (The book discusses Field's argument briefly (170–1), though it seems to me that this discussion does not focus on the argument's core.) Better theories of 'calling for explanation' can only help us understand Field's argument more deeply. But the absence of such theories does nothing to diminish its force. (Parallel: failing to find the correct philosophical theory of the nature of justice should not stop us from trying to promote justice. See Nolan 2016: 169 for relevant discussion.) Exploring connections between Field's contribution and epistemological challenges elsewhere in philosophy can also bring illumination (see, for instance, Enoch 2010).

If we accept that Field's argument does not refute platonism, but simply advances the debate by challenging the platonist to explain a particular phenomenon, then we would expect the responses to Field to consist of discussion of particular platonist proposals. This is not the case: there is a voluminous contemporary literature on Field's argument, but it mostly circles round the question of what (if anything) the argument shows, and how it relates to the modal epistemic conditions of safety and sensitivity (see Topey 2021 for an illuminating discussion). I think this is because of the prominence of the Undercutting Defeat interpretation of the argument. A more fruitful way forward is to see Field as Team Explanatory Power propose – as offering a relatively straightforward challenge – and to discuss various ways of trying to meet it.

I suggest that Field's challenge can be widened along various dimensions. According to platonists, plenty of non-mathematicians form mostly true mathematical beliefs as well, so it is reasonable to ask platonists to explain how these people manage to do that. I see no particular reason for avoiding concepts such as justification and knowledge here, so long as it's understood that the challenge does not appeal to any theories about justification or knowledge. A satisfying form of mathematical platonism would explain how people manage to form justified beliefs about abstract mathematical objects, and gain mathematical knowledge.

Quite a lot of work in philosophy of mathematics can be seen as a response to these challenges, even though it is not always explicitly framed as such. But it is notable that the literature often does not meet Field's challenges head on.

The Neo-Fregean philosophy of mathematics developed by Hale and Wright is an example. Here, the goal is to show a way in which, by making appropriate stipulations, we could come to acquire mathematical knowledge (see Wright 2001: 279–80). It is not clearly explained how to turn that into an account of the source of our actual mathematical knowledge, or even of our actual mathematical true belief.

Another example is work based on the Quinean idea that science is the fundamental source of mathematical knowledge. Quinean philosophy of mathematics tends to focus on the indispensability argument for the existence of abstract objects rather than on filling in the details of an epistemology for them.

Let me put those points in a slightly different way. There is a theoretical virtue which, I suggest, has been neglected in the recent debate over the epistemology of abstract objects. That virtue is strength. Other things being equal, a theory is more worthy of belief the more informative it is: that is, the more it rules out. As Williamson puts it: 'strength is a strength' (Williamson 2017: 337; see also Huber 2008). Once we remember the virtue of strength, we see that the discussion is currently out of balance: the epistemology of abstract objects tends to focus on relatively thinly specified theories. Giving the virtue of strength greater prominence would result in a diminished emphasis on Field's challenge itself and a greater emphasis on theory construction.

What sort of platonist epistemology might succeed in meeting Field's challenge? Let us work back from the challenge and see where we get. We want to explain the correlation between mathematicians' mathematical beliefs and the mathematical facts as the platonist conceives them. To do this, we could say that the beliefs and the facts are correlated because they both depend on some third thing. But it is simpler to say either that the beliefs depend on the facts or the facts depend on the beliefs. Since the latter threatens to compromise the objectivity of mathematics, the more natural step is to explore the former, and seek to explain how the beliefs could depend on the facts. Abstract objects are acausal, so the dependence must be acausal. Working back from Field's challenge, then, the obvious avenue to explore is whether the mathematical facts non-causally influence mathematical beliefs.

Metaphysicians of abstract objects are lucky: in recent years, the notion of non-causal influence has been studied extensively, often under the name of 'grounding'. (On grounding, Rosen 2010 is a good place to start. It is controversial whether the notion of grounding is in good standing: see Raven 2022, Section 'Skepticism and Anti-Skepticism'.) Elijah Chudnoff's work on intuition is a good example of how appeal to grounding can advance the debate. Chudnoff (2013) uses grounding to build an explanation of how intuitive experiences might make us aware of abstract objects. He argues that, just as our sense experiences can depend on concrete objects in our surroundings, so intuitive experiences can depend on abstract objects. These ideas merit much discussion. And we should also explore in detail other ways of using grounding to respond to Field.

It is natural to assume that non-causal explanations work by locating the explanandum in a network of non-causal dependence, as Chudnoff's explanation does. But that picture has been challenged: perhaps there are non-causal explanations that work in other ways, for example, Marc Lange's 'explanations by constraint' (Lange 2017). Understanding the different types of non-causal explanation can only help platonists trying to meet Field's challenge: the more sorts of non-causal explanation we can identify, the more types of explanation we might hope to offer of our mathematical accuracy. Each type provides a possible sort of answer for the platonist.

In short: Field's challenge does not refute platonism, but presents platonists with work to do. Whether they can meet the challenge remains to be seen.

5 Concluding Reflection

In a survey of the metaphysics of properties published in 1996, Alex Oliver found 'urgent, unanswered questions' (1) about the methodology of metaphysics: unclarity about what factors count for or against a theory, and unclarity about how to weight them against each other. Perhaps things are slightly better now, but we have at least seen how the metaphysics of abstract objects is held back by methodological problems. We do not agree over how metaphysical theories should relate to linguistics (Section 3.4) or to natural science (Section 3.5); we do not agree on which concepts are fit to be used in metaphysical theories (Sections 3.5 and 4.2); we do not agree on how to evaluate the parsimony of theories, nor on what sorts of parsimony are truth-conducive (Section 4.1). Is it any wonder, then, that we do not agree on whether abstract objects exist? The persistence of disagreement about this question, I suggest, is largely explained by persisting disagreement over what the rules are. (See Williamson 2007: 286–7 for related thoughts on persisting philosophical disagreement.)

My remarks are meant not as a counsel of despair, but as an invitation to more careful thought. The complex landscape of the abstract objects debate has many well-trodden paths, but there is plenty of territory that remains under-explored, or not explored at all. I can only hope that this Element has shown you some of the fascinating and valuable things to be found here, and pointed you in some promising directions.

References

Alston, W. (1958). Ontological commitments. *Philosophical Studies*, **9(1/2)**, 8–17. https://doi.org/10.1007/BF00797866.

Armstrong, D. M. (2004). *Truth and Truthmakers*. Cambridge: Cambridge University Press.

Baker, A. (2003). Does the existence of mathematical objects make a difference? *Australasian Journal of Philosophy*, **81(2)**, 246–64. https://doi.org/10.1080/713659635.

Baker, A. (2005). Are there genuine mathematical explanations of physical phenomena? *Mind*, **114(454)**, 223–38. https://doi.org/10.1093/mind/fzi223.

Baker, L. R. (1987). *Saving Belief: A Critique of Physicalism*. Princeton: Princeton University Press.

Balaguer, M. (1998a). Attitudes without propositions. *Philosophy and Phenomenological Research*, **58(4)**, 805–26. https://doi.org/10.2307/2653723.

Balaguer, M. (1998b). *Platonism and Anti-Platonism in Mathematics*. New York: Oxford University Press.

Balaguer, M. (2009). Fictionalism, theft, and the story of mathematics. *Philosophia Mathematica*, **17(2)**, 131–62. https://doi.org/10.1093/philmat/nkn019.

Baras, D. (2022). *Calling for Explanation*. New York: Oxford University Press. https://doi.org/10.1093/oso/9780197633649.001.0001.

Båve, A. (2015). A deflationist error theory of properties. *Dialectica*, **69(1)**, 23–59. https://doi.org/10.1111/1746-8361.12086.

Benacerraf, P. (1965). What numbers could not be. *Philosophical Review*, **74(1)**, 47–73. https://doi.org/10.2307/2183530.

Benacerraf. P. (1973). Mathematical truth. *Journal of Philosophy*, **70(19)**, 661–79. https://doi.org/10.2307/2025075.

Boyce, K. (2020). Mathematical surrealism as an alternative to easy-road fictionalism. *Philosophical Studies*, **177(10)**, 2815–35. https://doi.org/10.1007/s11098-019-01340-x.

Burgess, J. (1982). Epistemology and nominalism. In A. D. Irvine, ed., *Physicalism in Mathematics*. Dordrecht: Kluwer, pp. 1–15. https://doi.org/10.1007/978-94-009-1902-0_1.

Burgess, J. and Rosen, G. (1997). *A Subject with No Object: Strategies for Nominalistic Interpretation of Mathematics*. Oxford: Clarendon Press. https://doi.org/10.1093/0198250126.001.0001.

Chalmers, D. J. (2009). Ontological anti-realism. In D. J. Chalmers, D. Manley and R. Wasserman, eds., *Metametaphysics: New Essays on the Foundations of Ontology*. Oxford: Oxford University Press, pp. 77–129.

Chudnoff, E. (2013). *Intuition*. New York: Oxford University Press. https://doi.org/10.1093/acprof:oso/9780199683000.001.0001.

Clarke-Doane, J. (2017). What is the Benacerraf problem? In F. Pataut, ed., *New Perspectives on the Philosophy of Paul Benacerraf: Truth, Objects, Infinity*. Dordrecht: Springer, pp. 17–43. https://doi.org/10.1007/978-3-319-45980-6_2.

Cling, A. (1989). Eliminative materialism and self-referential inconsistency. *Philosophical Studies*, **56(1)**, 53–75. https://doi.org/10.1007/BF00646209.

Colyvan, M. (2001). *The Indispensability of Mathematics*. New York: Oxford University Press. https://doi.org/10.1093/019513754X.001.0001.

Colyvan, M. (2010). There is no easy road to nominalism. *Mind*, **119(474)**, 285–306. https://doi.org/10.1093/mind/fzq014.

Cowling, S. (2017). *Abstract Entities*. London: Routledge.

Daly, C. (2013). Psychology and indispensability. *Monist*, **96(4)**, 561–81. https://doi.org/10.5840/monist201396426.

Daly, C. and Liggins, D. (2010). In defence of error theory. *Philosophical Studies*, **149(2)**, 209–30. https://doi.org/10.1007/s11098-009-9346-1.

Daly, C. and Liggins, D. (2011). Deferentialism. *Philosophical Studies*, **156**, 321–37. https://doi.org/10.1007/s11098-010-9596-y.

Dever, J. (2008). Compositionality. In E. Lepore and B. Smith, eds., *The Oxford Handbook of Philosophy of Language*. Oxford: Oxford University Press, pp. 633–66. https://doi.org/10.1093/oxfordhb/9780199552238.003.0026.

Dorr, C. (2010). Of numbers and electrons. *Proceedings of the Aristotelian Society*, **110**, 133–81. https://doi.org/10.1111/j.1467-9264.2010.00282.x.

Edwards, D. (2014). *Properties*. Cambridge: Polity.

Enoch, D. (2010). The epistemological challenge to metanormative realism: How best to understand it, and how to cope with it. *Philosophical Studies*, **148(3)**, 413–38.

Felappi, G. (2014). 'In defence of sententialism'. *Dialectica*, **68(4)**, 581–603. https://doi.org/10.1111/1746-8361.12085.

Field, H. (1984). Review of *Frege's Conception of Numbers as Objects* by Crispin Wright. *Canadian Journal of Philosophy*, **14(4)**, 637–62. https://doi.org/doi:10.1080/00455091.1984.10716402.

Field, H. (1989). *Realism, Mathematics and Modality*. Oxford: Blackwell.

Field, H. (1998). Mathematical objectivity and mathematical objects. In S. Laurence and C. MacDonald, eds., *Contemporary Readings in the Foundations of Metaphysics*. Oxford: Blackwell, pp. 387–403.

Field, H. (2016). *Science without Numbers: A Defence of Nominalism*, 2nd ed. Oxford: Oxford University Press. https://doi.org/10.1093/acprof:oso/9780198777915.001.0001.

Fodor, J. A. (1987). *Psychosemantics: The Problem of Meaning in the Philosophy of Mind*. Cambridge, MA: MIT Press. https://doi.org/10.7551/mitpress/5684.001.0001.

Goldman, A. (1967). A causal theory of knowing. *Journal of Philosophy*, **64 (12)**, 357–72. https://doi.org/10.2307/2024268.

Goodman, N. and Quine, W. V. (1947). Steps toward a constructive nominalism. *Journal of Symbolic Logic*, **12(4)**, 105–22. https://doi.org/10.2307/2266485.

Hale, B. (1987). *Abstract Objects*. Oxford: Blackwell.

Hale, B. (2001a). Singular terms (1). In B. Hale and C. Wright, eds., *The Reason's Proper Study: Essays towards a Neo-Fregean Philosophy of Mathematics*. Oxford: Clarendon Press, pp. 31–47. https://doi.org/10.1093/0198236395.003.0002.

Hale, B. (2001b). Singular terms (2). In B. Hale and C. Wright, eds., *The Reason's Proper Study: Essays towards a Neo-Fregean Philosophy of Mathematics*. Oxford: Clarendon Press, pp. 48–71. https://doi.org/10.1093/0198236395.003.0003.

Hart. W. D. (1991). Benacerraf's dilemma. *Crítica: Revista Hispanoamericana de Filosofía*, **28(68)**, 87–103.

Hellman, G. (1989). *Mathematics without Numbers*. Oxford: Clarendon Press. https://doi.org/10.1093/0198240341.001.0001.

Hellman, G. (1998). Maoist Mathematics? *Philosophia Mathematica*, **6(3)**, 334–45. https://doi.org/10.1093/philmat/6.3.334.

Hellman, G. and Shapiro, S. (2019). *Mathematical Structuralism (Cambridge Elements: Elements in the Philosophy of Mathematics)*. Cambridge: Cambridge University Press.

Huber, F. (2008). Assessing theories, Bayes style. *Synthese*, **161**, 89–118. https://doi.org/10.1007/s11229-006-9141-x.

Huemer, M. (2009). When is parsimony a virtue? *Philosophical Quarterly*, **59 (235)**, 216–36. https://doi.org/10.1111/j.1467-9213.2008.569.x.

Jackson, F. (1977). Statements about universals. *Mind*, **86(343)**, 427–9.

Keller, J. A. (2017). Paraphrase and the symmetry objection. *Australasian Journal of Philosophy*, **95(2)**, 365–78. https://doi.org/10.1080/00048402.2016.1168457.

Kim, J. (2001). Lonely souls: Causality and substance dualism. In K. J. Corcoran, ed., *Soul, Body, and Survival: Essays on the Metaphysics of Human Persons*. New York: Cornell University Press, pp. 30–43. https://doi.org/10.7591/9781501723520-004.

Knowles, R. and Liggins, D. (2015). Good weasel hunting. *Synthese*, **192(10)**, 3397–412. https://doi.org/10.1007/s11229-015-0711-7.

Kovacs, D. (2021). How to be an uncompromising revisionary ontologist. *Synthese*, **198**, 2129–52. https://doi.org/10.1007/s11229-019-02196-8.

Lange, M. (2017). *Because without Cause: Non-Causal Explanations in Science and Mathematics*. New York: Oxford University Press.

Leng, M. (2010). *Mathematics and Reality*. Oxford: Oxford University Press. https://doi.org/10.1093/acprof:oso/9780199280797.001.0001.

Lewis, D. (1973). *Counterfactuals*. Malden: Blackwell.

Lewis, D. (1986). *On the Plurality of Worlds*. Malden: Blackwell.

Lewis, D. (1991). *Parts of Classes*. Oxford: Oxford University Press.

Liggins, D. (2008). Quine, Putnam, and the 'Quine–Putnam' indispensability argument. *Erkenntnis*, **68(1)**, 113–27. https://doi.org/10.1007/s10670-007-9081-y.

Liggins, D. (2010a). Epistemological objections to platonism. *Philosophy Compass*, **5(1)**, 67–77. https://doi.org/10.1111/j.1747-9991.2009.00259.x.

Liggins, D. (2010b). The autism objection to pretence theories. *Philosophical Quarterly*, **60(241)**, 764–82. https://doi.org/10.1111/j.1467-9213.2010.656.x.

Liggins, D. (2014). Abstract expressionism and the communication problem. *British Journal for the Philosophy of Science*, **65(3)**, 599–620. https://doi.org/10.1093/bjps/axt012.

Liggins, D. (2020). Against hermeneutic fictionalism. In B. Armour-Garb and F. Kroon, eds., *Fictionalism in Philosophy*, Oxford: Oxford University Press, pp. 81–102. https://doi.org/10.1093/oso/9780190689605.003.0005.

Liggins, D. (2021). Should a higher-order metaphysician believe in properties? *Synthese*, **199**, 10017–37. https://doi.org/10.1007/s11229-021-03234-0.

Lyon, A. (2012). Mathematical explanations of empirical facts, and mathematical realism. *Australasian Journal of Philosophy*, **90(3)**, 559–78. https://doi.org/10.1080/00048402.2011.596216.

Lyon, A. and Colyvan, M. (2008). The explanatory power of phase spaces. *Philosophia Mathematica*, **16(2)**, 227–43. https://doi.org/10.1093/philmat/nkm025.

MacBride, F. (1999). Listening to fictions: A study of Fieldian nominalism. *British Journal for the Philosophy of Science*, **50(3)**, 431–55. https://doi.org/10.1093/bjps/50.3.431.

Maddy, P. (1997). *Naturalism in Mathematics*. Oxford: Oxford University Press. https://doi.org/10.1093/0198250754.001.0001.

Maddy, P. (2005). Three forms of naturalism. In S. Shapiro, ed., *Oxford Handbook of Philosophy of Mathematics and Logic*. New York: Oxford

University Press, pp. 437–59. https://doi.org/10.1093/oxfordhb/9780195325928.003.0013.

Magidor, O. (2013). *Category Mistakes*. Oxford: Oxford University Press. https://doi.org/10.1093/acprof:oso/9780199572977.001.0001.

Malament, D. (1982). Review of *Science without Numbers* by Hartry H. Field. *Journal of Philosophy*, **79(9)**, 523–34. https://doi.org/10.5840/jphil198279913.

Markosian, N. (2004). A defence of presentism. In D. Zimmerman, ed., *Oxford Studies in Metaphysics*. Vol. 1. Oxford: Oxford University Press, pp. 47–82.

McCain, K. and Poston, T. (eds.) (2017). *Best Explanations: New Essays on Inference to the Best Explanation*. Oxford: Oxford University Press.

Melia, J. (1995). On what there's not. *Analysis*, **55(4)**, 223–9. https://doi.org/10.2307/3328390.

Melia, J. (1998). Field's programme: Some interference. *Analysis*, **58(2)**, 63–71. https://doi.org/10.1093/analys/58.2.63.

Melia, J. (2000). Weaseling away the indispensability argument. *Mind*, **109 (435)**, 455–79. https://doi.org/10.1093/mind/109.435.455.

Miller, K. (2012). Mathematical contingentism. *Erkenntnis*, **77(3)**, 335–59. https://doi.org/10.1007/s10670-012-9404-5.

Morrison, J. (2010). Just how controversial is evidential holism? *Synthese*, **173 (3)**, 335–52. https://doi.org/10.1007/s11229-008-9440-5.

Morrison, J. (2012). Evidential holism and indispensability arguments. *Erkenntnis*, **76(2)**, 263–278. https://doi.org/10.1007/s10670-011-9300-4.

Nolan, D. (1997). Quantitative parsimony. *British Journal for the Philosophy of Science*, **48(3)**, 329–43. https://doi.org/10.1093/bjps/48.3.329.

Nolan, D. (2016). Method in analytic metaphysics. In H. Cappelen, T. S. Gendler and J. Hawthorne, eds., *The Oxford Handbook of Philosophical Methodology*. Oxford: Oxford University Press, pp. 159–78. https://doi.org/10.1093/oxfordhb/9780199668779.013.16.

Oliver, A. (1996). The metaphysics of properties. *Mind*, **105(417)**, 1–80. https://doi.org/10.1093/mind/105.417.1.

Parsons, T. (1980). *Nonexistent Objects*. New Haven: Yale University Press.

Paseau, A. (2005). Naturalism in mathematics and the authority of philosophy. *British Journal for the Philosophy of Science*, **56(2)**, 377–96. https://doi.org/10.1093/bjps/axi123.

Pettigrew, R. (2008). Platonism and aristotelianism in mathematics. *Philosophia Mathematica*, **16(3)**, 310–32. https://doi.org/10.1093/philmat/nkm035.

Quine, W. V. (1960). *Word and Object*. Cambridge, MA: MIT Press.

Quine, W. V. (1969). Existence and quantification. In W. V. Quine, ed., *Ontological Relativity and Other Essays*. New York: Columbia University Press, pp. 91–113.

Quine, W. V. (1970). *Philosophy of Logic*. Englewood Cliffs: Prentice-Hall.

Quine, W. V. (1980). Logic and the reification of universals, In W. V. Quine, ed., *From a Logical Point of View*. 2nd ed. Cambridge, MA: Harvard University Press, pp. 102–29.

Raven, M. J. (2022). Metaphysical grounding. *Oxford Bibliographies Online*. https://doi.org/10.1093/OBO/9780195396577-0389.

Rosen, G. (1993). The refutation of nominalism (?). *Philosophical Topics*, **21** **(2)**, 149–86. https://doi.org/10.5840/philtopics199321221.

Rosen, G. (1999). Review of *Naturalism in Mathematics* by Penelope Maddy. *British Journal for the Philosophy of Science*, **50(3)**, 467–74. https://doi.org/10.1093/bjps/50.3.467.

Rosen, G. (2002). A study in modal deviance. In T. S. Gendler and J. Hawthorne, eds., *Conceivability and Possibility*. Oxford: Clarendon Press, pp. 283–307.

Rosen, G. (2009). Abstract objects. In E. N. Zalta, ed., *The Stanford Encyclopedia of Philosophy*. (Fall 2009 ed.). https://plato.stanford.edu/archives/fall2009/entries/abstract-objects/.

Rosen, G. (2010). Metaphysical dependence: Grounding and reduction. In B. Hale and A. Hoffman, eds., *Modality: Metaphysics, Logic, and Epistemology*. Oxford: Oxford University Press, pp. 109–36. https://doi.org/10.1093/acprof:oso/9780199565818.003.0007.

Rosen, G. and Burgess, J. (2005). Nominalism reconsidered. In S. Shapiro, ed., *The Oxford Handbook of Philosophy of Mathematics and Logic*. New York: Oxford University Press, pp. 515–35. https://doi.org/10.1093/oxfordhb/9780195325928.003.0016.

Saatsi, J. (2016). On the 'indispensable explanatory role' of mathematics. *Mind*, **125(500)**, 1045–70. https://doi.org/10.1093/mind/fzv175.

Schiffer, S. (2003). *The Things We Mean*. Oxford: Clarendon Press. https://doi.org/10.1093/0199257760.001.0001.

Sennet, A. and Fisher, T. (2014). Quine on paraphrase and regimentation. In G. Harman and E. Lepore, eds., *A Companion to W. V. O. Quine*. Oxford: Wiley-Blackwell, pp. 89–113. https://doi.org/10.1002/9781118607992.ch5.

Shapiro, L. (ed. and trans.) (2007) *The Correspondence between Princess Elisabeth of Bohemia and René Descartes*. Chicago: University of Chicago Press.

Sider, T. (1999). Presentism and ontological commitment. *Journal of Philosophy*, **96(7)**, 325–47. https://doi.org/10.2307/2564601.

Sider, T. (2013). Against parthood. In K. Bennett and D. W. Zimmerman, eds., *Oxford Studies in Metaphysics*. Vol. 8. Oxford: Oxford University Press, pp. 236–93. https://doi.org/10.1093/acprof:oso/9780199682904.003.0006.

Sjölin Wirling, Y. (forthcoming). Neutrality and force in Field's epistemological objection to platonism. *Inquiry*. https://doi.org/10.1080/0020174X.2022.2048689.

Skiba, L. (2021). Higher-order metaphysics. *Philosophy Compass*, **16**, 1–11. https://doi.org/10.1111/phc3.12756.

Sober, E. (1981). Evolutionary theory and the ontological status of properties. *Philosophical Studies*, **40(2)**, 147–76. https://doi.org/10.1007/BF00353787.

Sober, E. (2000). Quine's two dogmas. *Proceedings of the Aristotelian Society, suppl. vol.* **74(1)**, 237–80. https://doi.org/10.1111/1467-8349.00071.

Stanley, J. (2001). Hermeneutic fictionalism. *Midwest Studies in Philosophy*, **25 (1)**, 36–71. https://doi.org/10.1111/1475-4975.00039.

Stoljar, D. (2017). *Philosophical Progress: In Defence of a Reasonable Optimism*. Oxford: Oxford University Press. https://doi.org/10.1093/oso/9780198802099.001.0001.

Stump, E. and Kretzmann, N. (1981). Eternity. *Journal of Philosophy*, **78(8)**, 429–58. https://doi.org/10.2307/2026047.

Swain, M. (1998). Causal theory of knowledge. In E. Craig, ed., *Routledge Encyclopedia of Philosophy*. Vol. 5. London: Routledge, pp. 263–6. https://doi.org/10.4324/9780415249126-P004-1.

Swoyer, C. (1996). Theories of properties: From plenitude to paucity. *Philosophical Perspectives*, **10**, 243–64. https://doi.org/10.2307/2216246.

Szabó, Z. G. (2003). Nominalism. In M. J. Loux and D. W. Zimmerman, eds., *The Oxford Handbook of Metaphysics*. Oxford: Oxford University Press, pp. 11–45. https://doi.org/10.1093/oxfordhb/9780199284221.001.0001.

Tarski, A. (1983). On the concept of logical consequence. In J. Corcoran, ed., *Logic, Semantics, Metamathematics: Papers from 1923 to 1938*. Indianapolis: Hackett, pp. 409–20.

Topey, B. (2021). Realism, reliability, and epistemic possibility: On modally interpreting the Benacerraf–Field challenge. *Synthese*, **199**, 4415–36. https://doi.org/10.1007/s11229-020-02984-7.

van Elswyk, P. (2022). The linguistic basis for propositions. In C. Tillman and A. Murray, eds., *The Routledge Handbook of Propositions*. New York: Routledge, pp. 57–78. https://doi.org/10.4324/9781315270500-3.

von Solodkoff, T. (2014). Paraphrase strategies in metaphysics. *Philosophy Compass*, **9(8)**, 570–82. https://doi.org/10.1111/phc3.12150.

Walton, K. L. (1993). Metaphor and prop oriented make-believe. *European Journal of Philosophy*, **1(1)**, 39–57. https://doi.org/10.1111/j.1468-0378.1993.tb00023.x.

Wetzel, L. (2009). *Types and Tokens*. Cambridge, MA: MIT Press.

Williamson, T. (2007). *The Philosophy of Philosophy*. Malden: Blackwell.

Williamson. T. (2016). Abductive philosophy. *Philosophical Forum*, **47(3–4)**, 263–80. https://doi.org/10.1111/phil.12122.

Williamson, T. (2017). Semantic paradoxes and abductive methodology. In B. Armour-Garb, ed., *Reflections on the Liar*. Oxford: Oxford University Press. pp. 325–46. https://doi.org/10.1093/oso/9780199896042.003.0013.

Wright, C. (2001). On the philosophical significance of Frege's theorem. In B. Hale and C. Wright, eds., *The Reason's Proper Study: Essays towards a Neo-Fregean Philosophy of Mathematics*. Oxford: Oxford University Press, pp. 272–306. https://doi.org/10.1093/0198236395.003.0013.

Yablo, S. (1998). Does ontology rest on a mistake? *Proceedings of the Aristotelian Society, supp vol.* **72(1)**, 229–61.

Yablo, S. (2000). Apriority and existence. In P. Boghossian and C. Peacocke, eds., *New Essays on the a Priori*. Oxford: Clarendon Press, pp. 197–228. https://doi.org/10.1093/0199241279.003.0009.

Yablo, S. (2001). Go figure: A path through fictionalism. *Midwest Studies in Philosophy*, **25(1)**, 72–102. https://doi.org/10.1111/1475-4975.00040.

Yablo, S. (2002). Abstract objects: A case study. *Philosophical Issues*, **12(1)**, 220–40. https://doi.org/10.1111/j.1758-2237.2002.tb00068.x.

Yablo. S. (2005). The myth of the seven. In M. Kalderon, ed., *Fictionalism in Metaphysics*. New York: Oxford University Press, pp. 88–115.

Yablo, S. (2014). *Aboutness*. Princeton: Princeton University Press. https://doi.org/10.2307/j.ctt2tt8rv.

Acknowledgements

Many thanks to Ylwa Sjölin Wirling, Pablo Rychter, Rob Knowles, and an anonymous referee for their comments on a draft, and to Justina Berškytė for research assistance.

Cambridge Elements ⹀

Metaphysics

Tuomas E. Tahko
University of Bristol

Tuomas E. Tahko is Professor of Metaphysics of Science at the University of Bristol, UK. Tahko specializes in contemporary analytic metaphysics, with an emphasis on methodological and epistemic issues: 'meta-metaphysics'. He also works at the interface of metaphysics and philosophy of science: 'metaphysics of science'. Tahko is the author of *Unity of Science* (Cambridge University Press, 2021, *Elements in Philosophy of Science*), *An Introduction to Metametaphysics* (Cambridge University Press, 2015) and editor of *Contemporary Aristotelian Metaphysics* (Cambridge University Press, 2012).

About the Series

This highly accessible series of Elements provides brief but comprehensive introductions to the most central topics in metaphysics. Many of the Elements also go into considerable depth, so the series will appeal to both students and academics. Some Elements bridge the gaps between metaphysics, philosophy of science, and epistemology.

Cambridge Elements ≡

Metaphysics

Printed in the United States
by Baker & Taylor Publisher Services